THE CRETAN CHRONICLES
BLOODFEUD OF ALTHEUS

Felled by a treacherous blow in the deadly labyrinth of King Minos, your noble brother Theseus has died a hero's death. The spirits of your ancestors cry out from the halls of Hades for retribution, and Hermes, the messenger of the gods, is sent speeding to your side.

The message he brings sends YOU, Altheus, on a heroic voyage across the wild seas and lands of Ancient Greece to avenge your brother's death and rid the city of your birth of the scourge which threatens its survival. Mythical creatures and demons, powerful Amazons and scheming kings all endanger your passage, while the fickle gods embroil you in their intrigues and play games with your destiny.

With more than 600 references, this thrilling adventure features a new and complex combat system and the classic attributes of Might, Protection, Honour and Shame. The three parts of *The Cretan Chronicles* create a world of unparalleled authenticity and excitement which will stir the blood of any heroic adventurer.

John Butterfield, David Honigmann and Philip Parker are experienced gamers and are also the authors of *What is Dungeons and Dragons?* (Puffin Plus).

BLOODFEUD OF ALTHEUS

THE CRETAN CHRONICLES: 1

**John Butterfield, David Honigmann
and Philip Parker**

Illustrated by Dan Woods

PUFFIN BOOKS

Puffin Books, Penguin Books Ltd, Harmondsworth, Middlesex, England
Viking Penguin Inc., 40 West 23rd Street, New York, New York 10010, U.S.A.
Penguin Books Australia Ltd, Ringwood, Victoria, Australia
Penguin Books Canada Ltd, 2801 John Street, Markham, Ontario, Canada L3R 1B4
Penguin Books (N.Z.) Ltd, 182–190 Wairau Road, Auckland 10, New Zealand

First published 1985

Copyright © John Butterfield, David Honigmann, Philip Parker, 1985
Illustrations copyright © Dan Woods, 1985
All rights reserved

Made and printed in Great Britain by
Cox & Wyman Ltd, Reading

Typeset in Linotron Palatino
by Rowland Phototypesetting Ltd,
Bury St Edmunds, Suffolk

Except in the United States of America,
this book is sold subject to the condition
that it shall not, by way of trade or otherwise,
be lent, re-sold, hired out, or otherwise circulated
without the publisher's prior consent in any form of
binding or cover other than that in which it is
published and without a similar condition
including this condition being imposed
on the subsequent purchaser

CONTENTS

BACKGROUND AND RULES   7
  Might, Protection, Honour and Shame   8
  Combat   10
  Gods   14
  Equipment   15
  Taking a Hint   15
CHRONICLE SHEET   16

BLOODFEUD OF ALTHEUS   19

BACKGROUND AND RULES

'Theseus is dead,' replied Hermes. 'His body lies yet at the heart of the labyrinth of Minos. The spirits of your ancestors cry out from the halls of Hades, lusting for retribution. Aegeus, your noble father, mourns the loss of his strong-armed son. His spirit, fired with soul-searching anger, urges him on to revenge, but his feeble frame cannot undertake the task. It is you, amicable Altheus, who must journey far across the wine-dark sea, and destroy the scourge that threatens the city of your birth.' So it was that Hermes spoke, and in a wisp of smoke he vanished before you.

In this book you are Altheus, a Greek hero with an awesome mission to accomplish, striving against wild beasts and men, and seeking to win the favour of the gods in your quest. The journey will be difficult, but it is you who will determine your destiny. The book is laid out in paragraph format; at the end of each paragraph you will be given directions, which will determine the number of the paragraph to which you next turn. The paragraphs are set out in numerical order; you should not read a paragraph until you are sent to it from the one you have just read, or you will spoil the continuity and enjoyability of the adventure. If there is no destination given for you at the end of a paragraph, you are dead. In this case, you may start again at paragraph 1 with a new Altheus, all values at their initial value, all weapons and equipment as at the start, and all the gods' attitudes at Neutral.

You will need pencil, paper and dice to appreciate the travels of Altheus – your travels!

Might, Protection, Honour and Shame

Before you set out, there are a number of things it is necessary for you to know. Your mental state, your fighting skills and your relations with the supernatural and society are described in terms of four characteristics. These are Might, Protection, Honour, and Shame. Their values will change during the course of the game, so they must be recorded. For this purpose a blank Chronicle Sheet is provided (pp. **16–17**), which may be photocopied. Also marked on the Chronicle Sheet is a Wound Record track. This begins at Healthy, and as Altheus suffers injury it moves through Wounded and Seriously Wounded to Dead. Whenever Altheus or an opponent is hit, the Wound Record of that person is moved on one level from its previous value (Healthy/Unwounded to Wounded; Wounded to Seriously Wounded; Seriously Wounded to Dead). Death will in most cases be fatal, so take care! The Chronicle Sheet can also be used to record equipment carried, artefacts acquired on the journey, and whether Altheus is in favour or disfavour with the gods. In short, it details everything important about Altheus' condition and his relations with the outside world.

Altheus' Might value at a given time will nearly always be made up of a combination of his natural ability and the value of the strongest weapon he is carrying. This characteristic is used to determine how likely Altheus is to hit an opponent, should he find himself in combat. Altheus' natural Might is 4, but this will be supplemented whenever he is carrying a weapon.

Protection is made up of a combination of Altheus' inborn skill at dodging and the sum total of the armour he happens to be wearing. Altheus has inborn Protection of 10. Now suppose that he has greaves and a helmet. The greaves give 1 point of Protection, and the helmet 2. His total Protection value in this case is 13 (10+2+1). Protection is used mainly in combat, to determine how difficult an opponent will find it to strike at Altheus successfully.

Honour is all-important for Altheus. It determines his relations both with his fellow men and with his patron god or goddess. Without honour he will find himself an outcast. His patron deity will refuse to aid him when called on (not that this aid is in any case automatic); men will despise him and seek to do him ill. Altheus starts with an Honour value of 7. This may increase or decrease without restriction, but it may never decrease below 0. If it ever reaches 0, it may not increase again except through appeals to Zeus (see below) or by means of a special item described in the text. Honour is gained by victory in combat; it may be used up in appeals to the gods. Honour may also be used to gain a temporary increase in Might or Protection in combat.

Shame is another crucial concept in Bronze-Age Greece, the setting of this adventure. Shame, which initially has a value of 0, cannot be eradicated once acquired, except under exceptional circumstances (which will be detailed in the text). It is accumulated by such cultural *faux pas* as slaying one's opponent after he has surrendered, retreating ignominiously from a fair fight, or failing to perform heroic deeds. Such gross crimes as patricide, marrying one's own mother or failure satisfactorily to maintain one's armour will be penalized by a greater increase in Shame points. If Altheus' Shame ever rises above his Honour, he will be overwhelmed by the burden of his heroic conscience and he will either disembowel himself with a shortsword, if one is available, or be struck down by a thunderbolt from Olympian Zeus, father of the gods, and his spirit will go whining through the dark halls of Hades the life-destroyer. Resurrection is, in this case, specifically forbidden. If Shame exceeds Honour in the middle of a combat, no action is taken until the battle is completed. Thus the Honour he gains from victory may save him from this horrible fate.

Combat

Combat may occur in any encounter with a person or animal who is given combat abilities. You should always note these down on a piece of paper, not only for convenience, but also because you may well be sent to another paragraph. You should also keep a track of the Wound Record of an opponent. Combat is fought in a series of rounds called thrusts and counter-thrusts. Unless otherwise specified, Altheus will have the option of the first strike. If he performs some other action, such as appealing to the gods or using a magical item, his opponent will gain this initiative.

Altheus rolls two dice, and adds his natural Might and the value of his chosen weapon (note that if a weapon is given no Protection value or a piece of armour no Might value, this is because the relevant attribute is 0). If this total equals or exceeds the total Protection (natural ability + armour) of the opponent, Altheus has scored a hit. The Wound Record of the opponent is moved forward one stage. If Healthy, the opponent becomes Wounded; if Wounded, Seriously Wounded, and if Seriously Wounded, Dead, at which point the combat is over. On a dice roll of 11 or 12, Altheus will automatically hit his opponent, regardless of his Might or his opponent's Protection. Altheus may 'get lucky', even against the most formidable adversary. Conversely, on 2 or 3 he will automatically miss. His opponents fight in exactly the same manner, except that non-human opponents have no separate weapons or armour to be taken into consideration. If Altheus is fighting more than one opponent, the procedure is very slightly different. Altheus will fight them one by one, but each one's Might is increased by 1 for each surviving companion. For example, if Altheus fights three wolves (Might 2, Protection 12), the first wolf has effective Might 4, the second Might 3, and the last its own 2. In such multiple combats an opponent drops out when Seriously Wounded, and leaves the fight to his unwounded companions, if any; if all are Seriously Wounded, the text will give instructions as to what to do.

The fight continues until one side is dead or has surrendered. Once either Altheus or his opponent is Seriously Wounded, however, the injury will hamper fighting ability. Anyone suffering from such a wound will roll one die instead of two during combat. In this situation, a roll of 1 is an automatic miss, but a roll of 6 is not an automatic hit. If all participants in a combat are Seriously Wounded, then, in this case only, they are allowed to roll two dice, instead of one, until the end of the combat. Once a protagonist is Seriously Wounded, therefore, his chances of survival are very much less. Against a human opponent, in this situation, Altheus has the option of surrendering. The opponent will almost always accept this (the text will tell you whether or not he does), strip him of his strongest piece of armour and his strongest weapon (calculated according to their Might or Protection – the best has the highest value), and then let him go. Altheus must, however take 1 Shame point for such an action. If an opponent surrenders, Altheus must accept, or take 2 Shame points. He may then strip the opponent of any armour or weapon he wishes, bearing in mind that he may not wear more than one of any type of armour (a helmet, for example) although he may carry a spare. Again, the text will tell you whether or not a given opponent will surrender.

If Altheus is Healthy or Wounded (but not seriously), he may attempt to retreat. Any attempt will cost 1 Honour point, regardless of its outcome. A retreat is successful on a roll of 1 to 4, and fails on 5 or 6, unless specified in the text. A successful attempt will impose 1 point of Shame, and send you to the paragraph specified. Unsuccessful attempts rule out retreat for the remainder of the combat: the fight must continue until death or surrender.

Honour, as already mentioned, plays an important part in combat. Altheus may, if it is his strike, use Honour points temporarily to increase his Might. For example, if his Honour is 11, and his Might 9 (natural ability + axe), he may increase his Might to 11, for one roll only, by decreasing his Honour to 9. After the roll, the Might reverts to its former value, and the Honour points are lost for ever. Similarly, when it is his opponent's strike, Altheus may increase his Protection, for one roll only, by a corresponding reduction in Honour. He may do this as often as he likes, as long as he does not run out of Honour.

If Altheus is victorious in combat, he will receive Honour points. The text will specify how many points Altheus should receive as a result of a given combat. In addition, his Wound Record should be set back to Healthy at the end of any combat he survives.

Examples of Combat

Altheus, with a spear (Might 3, Protection 1) and a helmet (Protection 4), his Honour at 10 and Shame at 0, meets a lion (Might 5, Protection 15). Altheus' combat values are Might 7 (4 + 3) and Protection 15 (10 + 4 + 1).

Altheus decides to take no non-combat action, such as praying to the gods, and so strikes first. He needs an 8 to hit, because his Might of 7, plus a die roll of 8, is equal to the lion's Protection of 15. He rolls 6 and misses.

The lion needs 10 to hit. He rolls 11, so Altheus is Wounded. Altheus attacks again. This time he rolls 9, which hits. The lion is Wounded.

The lion again needs 10 to hit. He rolls 10, so Altheus is now Seriously Wounded, and only rolls one die in combat.

Altheus now needs 8 to hit, but this is impossible on one die. He therefore decides to use some Honour points. He transfers 3 points to his Might, which is now at a temporary level of 10. He now needs 5 to hit. He rolls 6: the lion is now Seriously Wounded. It has no Honour, and so cannot hit Altheus any longer. Altheus kills it in the next round, by using some more Honour, and he receives 6 points of Honour for slaying the lion. His Wound Record is returned to Healthy.

Later in this adventure, Altheus meets two Cretans, both Might 7, Protection 14. They carry clubs and shields. Altheus' values are as before: Might 7, Protection 15. He has acquired 1 Shame Point, but his Honour is now 12. The effective Might of the first Cretan is 8, because of his companion. Altheus, deciding the odds against him are too great, tries to retreat. He rolls 5 and fails, but still loses 1 point of Honour. The first Cretan now strikes, as Altheus has lost the initiative by attempting to retreat. He needs 7 to hit, but rolls 3, which is in any case an automatic miss.

Altheus rolls 9, which hits, as 9 plus his Might of 7 is greater than 14, the Cretan's Protection. The Cretan is Wounded.

The Cretan rolls 5, and misses.

Altheus rolls, and hits again. The Cretan is now Seriously Wounded, and drops out, leaving his companion to fight on. As he has no support, he fights at Might 7, Protection 14. He attacks Altheus, needing a roll of 8 or more to hit. He rolls 11, wounding Altheus.

Altheus rolls 5, missing the Cretan. He needs 7 to hit.

The Cretan rolls 3 and automatically misses.

Altheus would like to retreat now, but cannot, as he failed earlier on. Instead, he uses 5 points of Honour, to bring his Might up to 12. He needs 2 or more to hit. He rolls 2, but this is an automatic miss. Two of his Honour Points were wasted, as a roll of 2 or 3 misses, no matter what. His Honour is now at 6, and his Might back to 7.

The Cretan rolls 4, and again misses.

Altheus rolls 12, an automatic hit. The Cretan is now Wounded. The Cretan rolls 10. Added to his Might of 7, this makes 17, greater than Altheus' Protection, so he hits Altheus, who is now Seriously Wounded.

In desperation, Altheus uses 5 points of Honour to increase his Might to 12, so that he needs a roll of 2 on one die (only one, as he is Seriously Wounded) to hit. He rolls 4, and hits. Both Cretans are now Seriously Wounded.

At this point, Altheus rejoices, thinking that both Cretans will surrender. By turning to the appropriate paragraph, however, he finds that they are fanatical defenders of the labyrinth of Minos, and will never surrender. As neither side can score a hit – the Cretans are only using one die, and Altheus feels he cannot use any Honour as it would fall below his Shame, and if he failed to hit he would die – both sides are permitted to roll two dice instead of one. Even if Altheus wins

13

this combat his low Honour will cause problems; perhaps he will pray to Zeus . . .

Gods

The gods are a crucial part of Altheus' life. At the start of the adventure he must dedicate himself to one of Ares, Athena, Poseidon, Apollo, Aphrodite or Hera, and he must try to avoid angering any of the others. Presiding, enigmatic, over them all is Zeus, father of the gods, who will aid Altheus once in the adventure. Beneath this pantheon are many lesser gods, goddesses and spirits, whose anger is still to be avoided. In the case of a patron deity (who will be chosen later, in the course of the adventure), Altheus' standing is determined by his Honour. At certain points in the text, Altheus will be offered help by a deity; if it is his patron, he may expend the requisite amount of Honour (sometimes a random number) and accept the favour. If Altheus does not have enough Honour he will be referred back to the paragraph where the choice was offered, but will none the less lose 1 point of Honour. Once at 0, Honour cannot be regained, except by praying to Zeus, or by use of certain artefacts.

In the case of deities who are not his patron, Altheus is either in Favour (F), at Neutral (N), or in Disfavour (D). Initially, he will be at Neutral with all of the gods, except his patron, but this may change in the course of the adventure, as he performs actions which appease or anger the gods.

Altheus may pray to Zeus once during each adventure. This will have one of a number of effects, at Altheus' choice:

1. If he has been killed by any other means than Shame overtaking Honour, he may be resurrected, with all equipment, Shame of 0 and Honour of 1, at the paragraph indicated in the text. When Zeus saves you in this manner, do not be surprised if you find yourself moved to a nearby point in the same town or vicinity; this is simply divine Zeus' way of ensuring your safety.
2. He may simply gain 1 to 6 Honour points (roll one die).
3. If his Honour is at 0, he may have it set back to 1, and regain the ability to acquire Honour.

4. He may have the attitude of all the gods set back to Neutral, regardless of what they were.

Remember that the intervention of Olympian Zeus is very rare indeed, and may never be used more than once in an adventure, unless it is specifically offered in the text.

Equipment

Although you are a hero, you will start off lightly equipped, with only a club (Might 1, Protection 0) and no armour. During the course of the adventure you will acquire other pieces of equipment and should note these on the Chronicle Sheet. You may only carry one spare set of armour (in addition to any you may be wearing), and this will give you no extra Protection, but there is no limit to the amount of small items you may carry. This rule does not forbid the wearing of a breastplate and greaves and a helmet, etc., merely the wearing of two of any particular type of armour.

Taking a Hint

At times during the adventure, you may wish to perform non-standard actions. These will not be offered in the text, as this would give you a degree of foreknowledge granted only to the prescient. Instead, if you are at a paragraph with a number in italic type (i.e. *476* rather than 476), you may run the risk of adding 20 to the paragraph number and turning to that number; this process is known for convenience as 'taking a hint'. If there is no non-standard action at that point which a Bronze-Age hero would have thought of, you will pay a penalty in either Honour or Shame, or both, for trying to be ahead of your time.

Note that this option will never be explicitly offered in the text; you must remember it and use it when you see fit.

You are about to set off. If you have not already done so, record your initial values (Might 4, Protection 10, Honour 7, Shame 0) and your equipment (a club with Might 1, Protection 0) on the Chronicle Sheet.

Then turn to paragraph **1**, and good luck!

ALTHEUS CHRONICLE SHEET

	Natural	Best Weapon	
MIGHT	4	+	= ☐
	Natural	Armour	
PROTECTION	10	+ + + +	= ☐
HONOUR	7		
SHAME	0		

Weapons & Armour			Notes
	M	P	POSSESSIONS: Mother's Gem
CLUB	1	0	

ALTHEUS CHRONICLE SHEET

	Natural	Best Weapon	
MIGHT	4	+ 3	= 7
	Natural	Armour	
PROTECTION	10	+ 2 + 2 + +	= 14
HONOUR	7		
SHAME	0		

Weapons & Armour			Notes
	M	P	POSSESSIONS: Mother's Gem
CLUB	1	0	
SHIELD	0	2	NO HINT PENALTIES
BREASTPLATE	0	2	
SWORD	3	0	

The Gods

PATRON:

Favour *Disfavour*

Wound Record Track

HEALTHY   ☐ ☐ ☐ ☐ ☐ ☐
WOUNDED   ☐ ☐ ☐ ☐ ☐ ☐
SERIOUSLY
WOUNDED   ☐ ☐ ☐ ☐ ☐ ☐
DEAD   ☐ ☐ ☐ ☐ ☐ ☐

The Gods

PATRON: Apollo

Favour *Disfavour*

Dionysus   Hera
Aphrodite

Wound Record Track

HEALTHY   ☐ ☐ ☐ ☐ ☐ ☐
WOUNDED   ☐ ☐ ☐ ☐ ☐ ☐
SERIOUSLY
WOUNDED   ☐ ☐ ☐ ☐ ☐ ☐
DEAD   ☐ ☐ ☐ ☐ ☐ ☐

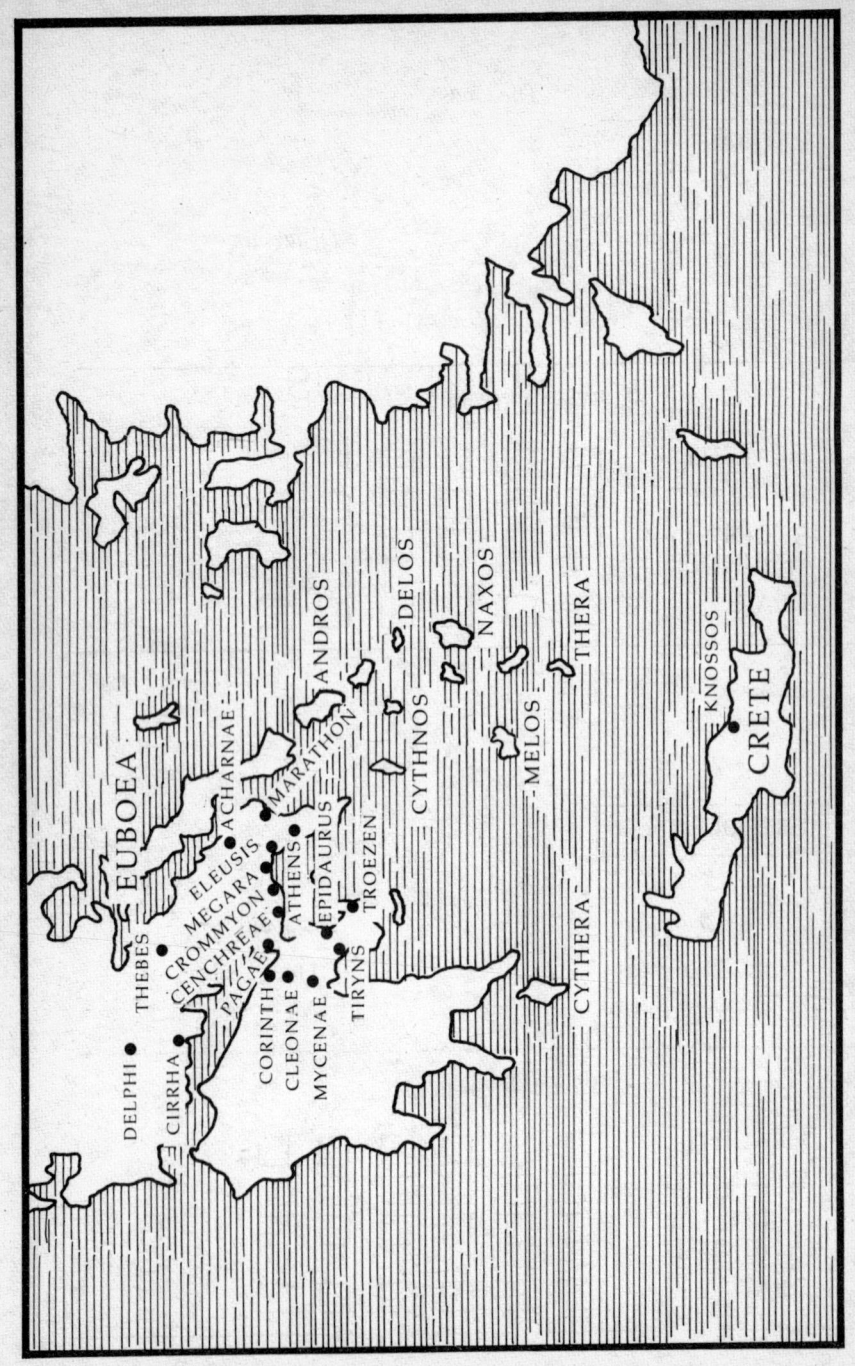

BLOODFEUD
OF ALTHEUS

1

Trembling with terror at the tale of Hermes, you rush out of your cottage and into the fields. You search for your mother, Aethra, and find her huddled under a spruce tree tending the goats. In haste you blurt the words of the god.

'My son,' replies your mother, 'the words of the god fill me with sorrow, but they are true, for the gods never lie. You must follow the orders of the winged messenger. Travel to violet-crowned Athens and seek for your father Aegeus. Take with you my jewel, for it was once your father's, and he will surely recognize it. But first visit Passes, High Priest of Troezen, and take what advice he can give you. Good luck, my son: prove worthy of your noble father and your dead brother.'

Having spoken, she turns away lest you catch sight of her tears. You linger a moment, then, with the jewel clasped firmly in your hand, you rush away down the hillside into the town. It is dawn, and rosy-fingered Eos has only just tinged the horizon with red. The streets of Troezen are empty, save for a handful of scurrying slaves already about their masters' business, and you come quickly to the temple. The High Priest greets you; he already knows of your errand.

'Altheus, before you lies a great journey to lands of which you have never even dreamt. Many dangers await you; without the aid of a god you cannot prevail. Choose now a patron god or goddess to guide and help you.

'Grey-eyed Athena offers you the gift of wisdom; Ares, god of war, offers strength. If beauty tempts you, think of Aphrodite. Apollo, the archer god, controls the gift of prophecy, while Hera, queen of the gods, has influence over Zeus. Your travels are sure to take you across seas and oceans, and these are Poseidon's province. Choose now one of these six to aid you, and pay them homage. Good luck, Altheus son of Aegeus.'

For Aphrodite, turn to **42**.
For Ares, turn to **71**.
For Poseidon, turn to **117**.
For Athena, turn to **168**.
For Hera, turn to **203**.
For Apollo, turn to **352**.

2

The road is hard and you are soon tired. As you struggle up a rocky mountain path, a man and a woman ride past on a horse, deep in conversation. As they gallop on, the dust makes you splutter, but they are out of sight before you can react. Eventually you reach the top of the hill, and, for the first time in your life, can look down into the valley beyond. It is fertile and inviting. You can see high-walled Tiryns in the distance and, a little nearer and to the east, Epidaurus sacred to Asclepius the healer. You drink deeply from the wineskin and press on down the hillside.

The path forks: will you go left (turn to 309) or right (turn to 410)?

3

The sun, now well above your home far off in Troezen, throws gentle light down on the earth below. Its warming rays play on the leaf-filled trees. The way out of Cleonae climbs gently to the crest of the foothills. Your legs, now fresh and eager for the journey, make light work of the ascent. As you reach the top, you gasp at the panorama below. To your left the Gulf of Corinth opens out in a vast expanse of wine-dark water. At its head lies the city of Corinth, standing like a watchtower, vigilant over the sea, in case the pirates come to carry off the crops and lay waste the well-stocked villages. At the foot of the hills to the right is little Cenchraea, sister of Corinth, as the moon is of the sun. Beyond the harbour the Saronic Gulf reaches out almost to Athens, city of the owl-eyed goddess. Between the waters the Isthmus links the Isle of Pelops with the wilder lands beyond. You ponder your choice between bustling Corinth (go to 152), and quiet seafaring Cenchraea (go to 589).

4

You take the bowl, and tip its contents into the water. It forms a soggy mass and causes the water to overflow on to the table. The crowd recoils in horror at your action. Go to 120.

5

Your heroic stature reduced to a mere cipher, the gods do not even bother to strike you down, but let you eke out your miserable existence in a life of petty crime, from which you are unable to escape.

6

Take 1 Shame point for your cowardice. If your patron is Ares turn to **157**. If not, turn to **228**.

7

You knock once on the pine door, but nobody replies. You knock again, harder, and this time a serving-maid opens the door. She looks surprised to see you, and calls out to a massively built woman, who wears a woollen apron. She is clearly in charge of the kitchen, and when she catches sight of you, she demands to know who you are. Do you reply 'Altheus' (**280**), or 'Pyraphas' (**604**)?

8

The queen of the Amazons sits cross-legged on the dusty floor, her leopardskin fastened at the shoulder with a golden brooch.

'Here,' you say, 'is what you seek. Go now from the Athenian shores and while all-seeing Zeus scans the earth with immortal eye, let not your great-oared ships make landing on our beaches.'

Antiope accepts the object from your hands, cradles it in her arms for a moment, and then directs her gaze at you. 'Let the Athenians also beware; for if they come again to the Amazonian shores we will be prepared, and the young men of Attica will perish on a foreign shore, as a flower shrivels up in the burning heat of the summer, and the garden is bare. Yet in return for your heroic generosity I will aid you a little. I know you travel to Crete. There seek out an Amazon named Lembra, and say you are Antiope's friend.'

With this she unpins the brooch from her shoulder, and hands it to you, so Lembra can recognize you. You do not stay, but go quickly back to Aegeus to tell him that there is peace between the two nations. Have 5 Honour points for preventing the war. Go to **25**.

9

After a short time the next race begins, and it is obvious that the red team is doing spectacularly poorly, as a boy racing against his elders finds himself outmatched. The blue team laps the red driver, but the latter in his inexperience swerves the wrong way, and ends the race for both of them. Soon the yellow chariot has a commanding lead, and the race comes to an anticlimactic conclusion.

You go to bed, tired of the Acharnian chariot races. Next morning you wake, and set out refreshed for Athens (**474**).

10

'Stranger,' booms one of the satyrs, as you step forward, 'come, join our revels.' A goblet is thrust into one of your hands as the music starts afresh. A nymph slips her hand into yours, and the dancing begins afresh. The hot blood pounds in your veins, and as the hours pass you drink deeply of the vine's fruit, and forget yourself in the blissful oblivion of Dionysus. Go to **232**.

11

The god fills the bull with a divine frenzy, and it sets upon the men. Suddenly afraid at the charging of the beast, they drop their javelins and rush back to Cirrha and beyond, as the farmer who has trodden upon a snake unawares recoils and is afraid, runs away, and leaves his plough untended, and his corn for the black crows to pick at. You may pick up one of the javelins for yourself. It is normally Might 1, Protection 0, but you may, as your first action in a combat, throw it, and then engage in normal combat, still having the first strike, if you want it. So long as you defeat your opponent, you retrieve the javelin. You carry on into Cirrha. Go to **92**.

12

You are still thirsty, but think to yourself how sensible it was not to have drunk from the waters of Mycenae, filled as they are with dust from the now crumbling walls, and the waste of the city. You stroll through the back alleys, taking advantage of the welcome shade offered by the close-built streets. Go to **73**.

13

You walk on down the road for many hours. Ahead, in the centre of the plain, a town stands whitely, baking in the morning sun. Above, an eagle circles and swoops. Then it rises into the air again, a small mouse clasped in its talons. Soon, you reach the town, and discover that you were correct. The place is Thebes.

Quickly, you enter the gates of the city. Even as you do so, you wish you were elsewhere. The very ground is sticky, and the smell of unwashed, unwanted beggars assails your nostrils. A small boy runs up and tries to take your boots. He is soon joined by many others of his ilk. Wrinkling your features in unashamed disgust, you press on through the grimy, unlovely alleys. Your belly pleads for food, but your head urges you to quit this foul place. If you eat, go to **238**; if you try to leave the town hungry, go to **134**.

14

When you turn the final corner, the roar of the crowd blocks off everything else, just as wives and children hail the conquering warriors back from the wars. You rein your chariot to a halt, and leap lightly out. Already the townsfolk have surged forward, and now raise you shoulder-high. On your head is placed the victor's laurel wreath. You may have 5 Honour points for your victory. You wander around the town, feted by Acharnians, and show great *laevendia*.

Eventually you return to your inn, where you slump insensate into sleep. Soon the innkeeper brings you your breakfast, and then you are on your way to Athens (**474**).

15

The dog growls menacingly as you pass by. Just when you think you are safely away, it rushes out, and the chain snaps as it lunges towards you. It sinks its savage teeth deep into your ankle. You kick it, and manage to drive it off. It goes whimpering back to its master's house. Go to **440**.

16

As you approach the spot you find that you were mistaken. There is no place to spend the night. Suddenly two men emerge from the shadows and bar the way in front of you. You are about to spring to the attack, when you feel a sharp blow at the back of the neck. You slump unconscious to the ground, and when you awake you find that your money-bag and your weapons have been stolen. The armour you were wearing (if any) has not gone, although attempts have been made to loosen it. You feel in your tunic and find with a sigh of relief that the money and possessions stored there have not been taken. Lose 1 Honour point for being mugged. Go to **331**.

17

The storeroom is cold and dank. In the corners you can hear the chittering of rats as they gnaw away at the grain supply of Thebes. Soon you fall unconscious, asleep. Your sleep is troubled, and you awaken frequently, sweating and breathless, like a runner who has just finished last in a race, for whom there is no victor's wreath.

At dawn the door is opened, and you are pulled out from the heap of grain where you rested. The king has been wounded by an assassin, but will not die, so you are free to go.

Tired and terrified, you go quickly to the palace gates and collect your weapons, afraid lest the king die, when you would surely be executed. Go to **134**.

18

No one else takes any notice, and the man stumbles away from the curtain. At length the Pythia ceases her ecstatic wailing, and the priest returns.

'Altheus,' he says, 'the clear-sighted god has spoken thus:

> *"If peace it is you seek, drink the queen's health.
> If not then strife will be your only wealth."'*

You say farewell. Wondering at the words of the god, and having first retrieved your weapons, you set off down to Thebes. Go to **191**.

19
You take some of the seed from the bowl and scatter it on the crowd. It blows in the wind, and the people shout out, eager to catch even a grain. Seeing that you have chosen rightly, you continue until the bowl is half empty. Go to **212**.

20
Without warning, two black-cloaked brigands leap out of the bushes, and before you have a chance to react, one of them has stabbed you in the thigh. You are Wounded. Go to **462**.

21
Procrustes, now Seriously Wounded, goes berserk rather than surrender. He only rolls one die, and abandons his axe, but his combat values change to Might 12, Protection 5. If you kill him, go to **315**; if you die, but Zeus saves you, go to **263**.

22
No Greek hero should feel fear so soon after leaving the halls of his ancestors. Take 1 point of Shame and go back to **2**.

23
You spend a miserable night, shivering in the cold, dark street. In the morning many early-risers pass by, jeering, as they go to their toils in the fields of waving corn. For this dishonourable place of rest for the night, you lose 1 Honour point. Go to **3**.

24
You plunge the dagger into his neck. His blood spurts out like water from a shattered vessel. His body jerks in a final spasm, and is still. You have slain a king. Horrified by the enormity of your crime, you must have 7 Shame points. You may however take his sword. It has Might 3, Protection 1.

Just as you unsheathe the sword you hear noises. You look out of the window, see shadows moving in the courtyard and hear rushing footsteps.

Do you try to escape out of the window, into the courtyard (**472**)?

Or do you leave by the door (**249**)?

25
Back to the house of your father you go, pride in your heart. In the great hall the nobles of Athens are once again gathered. You explain the success of your mission, and they cheer, applauding you, just as if you came a conquering hero, having laid low Athens' enemies and left their corpses for the dogs. Go to **441**.

26
You recognize the woman as Hera, your white-armed patron. Go to **543**.

27
You take the urn, and in your attempt to sprinkle the water on the crowd, it all rushes out and soaks two stalwart citizens standing at the front of the crowd. With almost deafening shouts of anger, they rush up the steps. The rest of the mob follows them, screaming its anger. The taller of the two men grabs your arms before you have a chance to draw a weapon,

and the other kicks you viciously in the stomach. You fall doubled up, and a single blow connects with your head. If you have not yet prayed to Zeus, now you must do so (you will find yourself at paragraph **138**). The lynch mob tear at your limbs, and not soon enough does grim-faced Hades sunder your spirit from its battered flesh.

28

The sea becomes deathly calm, and the seagulls seem to cease their constant crying. From the uttermost west he comes, Talos, the giant of bronze. God-made, he almost runs through the water, gigantic sword in hand. Muscles not made of flesh ripple, and his mouth seems to form itself into an inhuman grin. He cannot speak, but roars his defiance in a strange metallic clanging.

You must face Talos in combat. He is Might (*)14, Protection 18. You have no retreat.

If you hit Talos three times, go to **617**.

If you surrender, go to **443**.

If you die, go to **174**.

29

Zeus' healing touch revives you, and your limbs, rent by the mighty jaws of Poseidon's serpent, are knit together anew. You must carry on the fight. You can either remain on deck (go to **484**), or plunge into the sea to face your foe (go to **361**).

30

As the rider disappears behind you, you clamber out of the ditch, but then the horseman comes riding back towards you, shouting, and you can tell that it is, in fact, a woman. Take 1 point of Shame and go to **107**.

31

Weighed down by armour and a coil of rope you thought to grab as you plunged into the sea, you sink. You gasp and struggle, frantically trying to free yourself. Above the rushing of the water, you hear the laughter of the captain, crew and fourteen Athenians. In your distress you are relieved when someone grasps hold of you and pulls you out from the death-bringing waves. To your embarrassment, it is the woman who was in the boat. She has steered it away from the rocks to come and rescue you. Have 2 Shame points.

If Aphrodite is your patron, go to **587**.
Otherwise, go to **395**.

32

Taking the corn seed from the bowl, you scatter it far into the crowd, your cast made stronger by the fresh wind blowing from behind. In its joy the crowd scrabbles to collect the sacred grain, symbol of the new-born fertility of the earth. Go to **300**.

33

Down to the deck you fall, your possessions storm-scattered into the dark depths. You must lose all your possessions save the documents for Minos (if you have them), anything gained from Antiope, a weapon of your choice, a piece of armour of your choice, and one other item from your Chronicle Sheet, which must not be arms or armour. Go to **363**.

34

You cry out to the sea god. 'If ever you have heard me from the depths of the waters, help me now and deliver us from this creature of your realm.' There is a tremendous rumbling beneath the waves and the waters begin to twist and turn in a whirlpool. The serpent is sucked down into the vortex, back into the inky-dark regions whence it came, denied its glory in the strong encounter.

You have been saved, but now Poseidon is Neutral to you. Go to **349**.

35

Someone urges you to save her, but it is too late. The crew stand aghast at your failure to save the woman from black-hearted Fate. Have 4 Shame Points, and turn to **608**.

36

Inside, it is worse than even the wretched exterior suggested. There is a powerful smell of rotting food and unwashed locals. Despite being nearly overcome by nausea, you step up to the bar.

'Innkeeper,' you shout, 'a room for the night!'

At the far end of the bar the innkeeper, a grossly fat, cowardly looking man, continues to ignore you. Beside you an old man, with bare feet, speaks.

'Son, if I were you, I would leave at once, for Epidaurus is beset by foul bandits, terrorizing the temple of Asclepius the healer. Go quickly, for they will likely kill strangers or, perhaps, since you hold yourself as a hero, you could rid our town of this curse,' he adds, with sarcasm heavy in his voice.

The innkeeper has now come over, and proffers you a key to an upstairs room.

Do you pay him and take the key to the room, going upstairs for long-fingered Sleep to brush closed your weary eyelids (go to **199**)?

Or do you react to the old man's taunt at once, and seek the bandits (go to **508**)?

37

You rush into the attack, but your opponents are also swift. They draw daggers from the folds of their cloaks and defend themselves. The plotters are Might 6 (5 + 1 for a Dagger), Protection 13 (12 + 1 for a Bearskin). Remember the rules about fighting multiple opponents.

If both of your opponents are Seriously Wounded, go to **301**.

If you surrender, go to **450**.

If you die and are saved by Zeus, go to **134**.

If you retreat out of the inn, and away into Thebes, go to **134**.

38

You have got away with your crime. You have in your tunic the stolen loaf. You move quickly away from the market, fearful of being noticed even now. You are not particularly hungry;

indeed, on reflection, you can see no reason why you committed this senseless deed. You could eat the loaf, and destroy the evidence (go to **346**), or you could try to sell the loaf to a passer-by (go to **594**).

39
You find yourself climbing up a steep slope. The ascent seems endless, but at last you reach a flat place. Your legs are pulled from under you and now each of your limbs is held. You plead for forgiveness, but the only response is laughter. Suddenly your captor's grip is gone. For one moment you try to stand, but find no ground beneath you. You claw wildly at the air as you fall, faster and faster. Not even Zeus will save you from death now.

40
You pause for a moment, and then carry on, unhindered, into the city itself. You must find the way to the palace, but do not know how to. Ahead of you are grand houses, built in stone, the abodes of some great lords of the city, but not large enough to be the house of your father. To either side of these, lesser houses of mud-baked brick block further progress into the city.

You could carry on along this road to the left (**90**), or to the right (**580**). Alternatively, you could ask someone the way to the palace (**426**).

41
You can, however, disarm him and take him to the city authorities for judgement. You may take his axe (Might 5, Protection −3) and continue on your way next morning. Go to **263**.

42
You offer prayers to Aphrodite and then start on the journey to Athens, where your father is king. The road is hard desert, and the sun beats down relentlessly. After many more hours your feet grow weary and your sight grows dim. In the distance

ahead, you see a lone horseman galloping towards you. Do you hide in the ditch until he goes past (turn to **30**), or carry on as normal (turn to **107**)?

43

The priest smiles, and the smile is as the frost that takes hold on the field of golden corn, and the harvest is lost. Go to **126**.

44

If you are in Favour with Poseidon, then any roll of 5 will advance your favoured horse by 1 space, if you spend 1 Honour point. If Poseidon, the horse lord, is your patron then the horse on which you bet advances 1 space on a roll of 5, without the need to spend any Honour. Return to **391**.

45

Tiryns seems as uninteresting as your journey there. There are a few drunken brawls, but nothing a hero would get involved in. The day's travel begins to sap the strength from your legs, and you feel that you must rest. You look for a place to spend the night. Go to **200**.

46

'Altheus,' the woman says, 'it is I, your patron, Hera, whom you forsake so easily.' You look, and it is true: on the banks of the river stands the immortal queen. You struggle back to the shore and the goddess speaks once more. 'Too late for that,' she says. 'My gift is that Zeus is my husband. When you call on me, I can entreat my husband on your behalf, but since you have offended me, I shall not listen before you have sacrificed to me.' You may be saved by Zeus one extra time, but only after you have sacrificed 6 Honour points to Hera (and deducted them from your total). Go to **146**.

47

The bull gores you to death, but Olympian Zeus mends your bloodied limbs. You seem to hear the god himself speaking to you. 'I have saved you now, but to merit the gift of life, you must kill the bull.'

You must carry on with the fight. If you win, turn to **225**. Should you wish to retreat, turn to **515**.

48

As Talos strides towards you, his feet crashing down on the sea floor like the battering-ram that is hurled against the city gate and must in the end prevail, you notice on his right ankle a circular mark, as if a hole has been plugged. Perhaps this is the spot from which his ichor, his life-blood, flows! You plunge into the water. It is shallow, coming only up to your waist, and soon you are at the spot.

Talos is Might (*)14, Protection 18. You can try to pry the plug open (go to 365), or you can fight Talos.
If you hit him three times, turn to 617.
If you surrender, turn to 443.
If you die, turn to 174.

49

The city of Athens laid out below you is magnificent indeed. How much greater, you muse to yourself, must the entire earth seem to Zeus sitting on his Olympian throne. Yet Athens must be by far its fairest city, second only to the divine realm of the gods. Temples to all the gods lie below, evidence of Athens' devotion to the Olympians, but naturally the greatest of them all is that to Athena. To one side of this, on the outskirts of the city, lies the palace, the sun reflecting off the walls, damp from the rain of the storm earlier. You hurry down the hill, eager to reach your destination. Go to 236.

50

Aegeus' expression turns from one of joy to seriousness. 'This is an opportune time that you come, for Athens is beset by an ancient peril. Each year, we must send seven young men and seven girls to sate the appetite of the Cretan Minotaur. You, my son, must be our emissary. I shall send you to Crete with messages and a gift for King Minos, demanding that this terrible tribute be relaxed, and that he accept gold and silver rather than the flower of our youth; for of the one we have abundance, of the other little, and beyond price. If he will not accept, there will be war between our states.'

General Etekon, a bluff, bearded man, interjects: 'And you must bring back all the information you can, in case the worst occurs.' Yet in his bloodshot eyes you can see that this is a prospect he rather hopes for than fears.

'Come,' continues Aegeus, and walks over to a doorway leading out from the great hall. 'I will draw up the documents.'

Do you wait in the hall for Aegeus to complete his task (364)?

Or do you leave the gathered assemblage of Athens' nobility behind, and follow your father (123)?

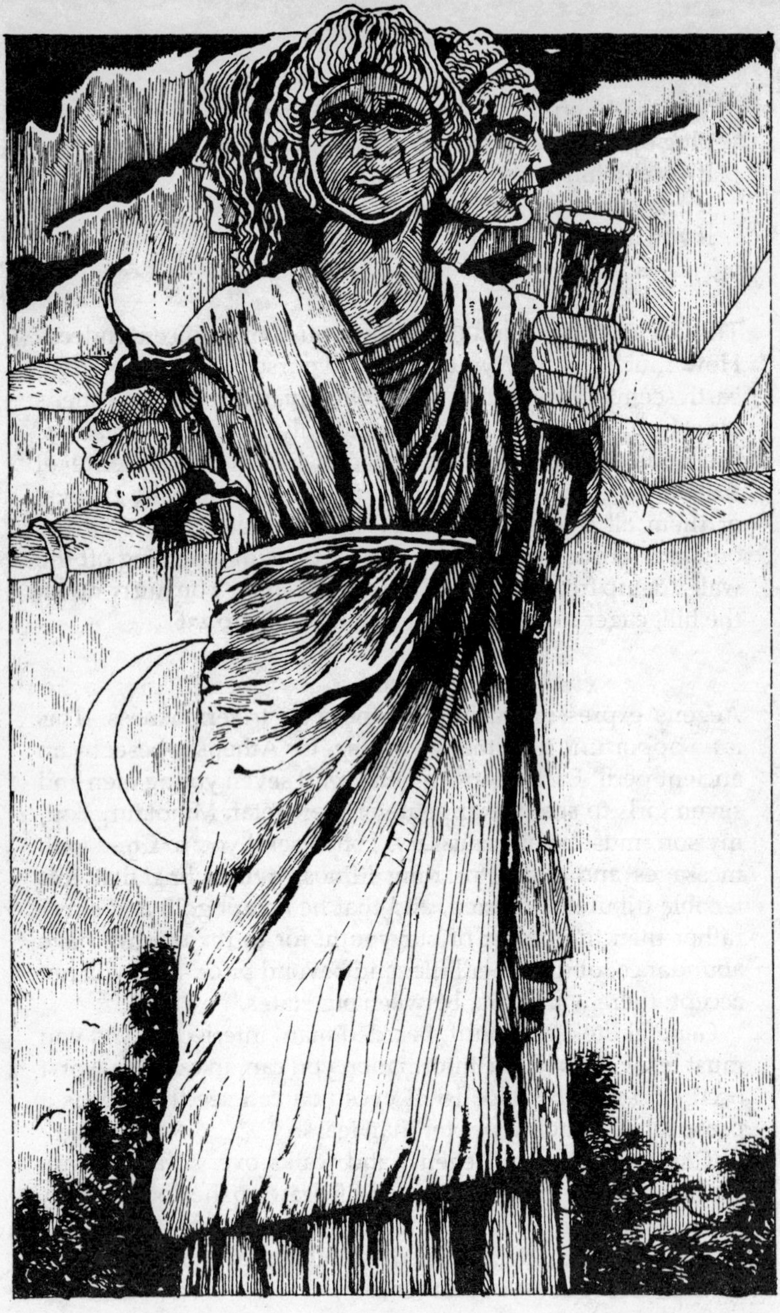

51

Quickly on your way from the disease-ridden town of Pagae, you come to a fork in the road. Placed just where it begins, is the triple-formed statue of Hecate, queen of the underworld, and goddess of night, one head pointing in each direction. In one of her six hands, she carries a headless jet-black puppy. In another she holds a torch. You may pass the statue to the right, on towards Eleusis (go to **86**), or to the left and Delphi (go to **478**).

52

You lie awake for a time considering the long journey that lies ahead of you. You have travelled far from Troezen, and learnt much, yet your task is not half done, and you know it will be long before the words of the god Hermes cease to echo down the chambers of your life. At last, you sleep. Go to **411**.

53

It is hopeless. There are now just two of you left clinging to the floating wood. Your companion loses his grip on the bench he is holding and does not again emerge from the water beneath. You feel your strength ebbing fast, and just as you are about to give in, and offer your soul to grim Hades, your patron appears and offers you succour if you will only show your faith. To save yourself you must lose 4 Honour points. If you cannot afford this, your only hope is to pray to Zeus, if you have not already done so. In either case, go to **247**. If not, then your body will float, untended, unburied, and you will wander, a homeless shade, on the banks of the River Lethe.

54

Tired and angry you toss the pot into the corner where it shatters into a thousand pieces. The labyrinth and Crete seem so far away, and you bang at the door, demanding to be released. The guard says nothing, and at length you cease. Perhaps your patron will release you. Turn to **569**.

55

Faster than the arrow that leaps from the bow into the flying hart, the god himself appears to you. 'Altheus, you are in grave danger. The innkeeper Procrustes makes it his gruesome duty to fit all of his guests to the bed, with an axe if necessary. Hide behind the door and you may surprise him. But hurry!' Go to **272**.

56

A blinding light fills the air for a brief moment, and then you find that you can see no more. You shriek in pain, as the bird caught in flight by the archer's arrow cries out briefly, before it plummets to the ground. You feel strong arms grip you from behind, and you are led away quickly. You stumble often, and are pushed along roughly by your captors. Go to **39**.

57

You pass several other bands of pilgrims, but you do not speak to any of them, anxious to be on your way as fast as possible. You ignore, also, the hostels which line the route at regular intervals, places where travellers may gain some respite from the hardships of the road. You realize you are drawing closer to Delphi, as the number of pilgrims on the road increases, so that always ahead of you some figure treads the road. Night is falling as you approach the town of Cirrha. Go to **339**.

58

You ponder to yourself what part the water plays in the ceremony.

You could drink the water (**435**).
You could use the water to quench the flame (**306**).
You could sprinkle water on the corn (**101**).
Or you could sprinkle it on the crowd (**27**).

59

You hail the strong-limbed crew, and explain your plan. There are several ways you could proceed. One sailor has a short barbed spear to throw at the cows, and sever their unknowing lives. If you choose this, go to **535**. Alternatively you could try to wrestle a cow down unarmed. If you do this, turn to **565**.

60
You are in Favour with Hera. You may have 2 Honour points. Go to **294**.

61
Searching the house, you find a breastplate (Protection 2). Go to **263**.

62
For a second the gathered crowd pauses. Seeing their indecision, you exhort them once more to save the men. 'Do not defile the city by this dreadful deed,' you cry. The crowd can see that you are obviously some great hero, and take heed of your words. They disperse silently, and the two men are left alone. They thank you gratefully, and say that they will now head out of Athens for some friendlier town. Go to **394**.

63
With a cry of 'Stop, robbers!' you spring into the attack, but they are unworthy opponents, and by the time you reach the stall only one remains, having tripped over the fruit spilled from the stall in his panic. Your blow strikes home, and he is Wounded, still on the ground. He has Might 6, Protection 10.

If he is Seriously Wounded, turn to **438**.

If you surrender to him, turn to **149**.

If you die and are saved by Zeus, turn to **86**.

If you retreat, go to **86** (remember the Shame point, for successfully retreating, in addition to the 1 Honour penalty for trying to retreat).

64

Determined to foil this evil plot, you stay a moment considering the choices to which grim-hearted Lachesis points with her staff.

You could go to the palace, and warn the king of the plans against his life (**506**).

Or do you try to tackle the men yourself (**372**)?

65

There is nothing to be afraid of yet. Nobody takes any notice of you, but you lose 1 Honour point for being timid, rather than the great-hearted hero your brother was. Go back to **45**.

66

As you ride along, the lady reveals herself as the goddess Aphrodite. 'You're a good boy, Altheus,' she simpers. 'You have shown trust in beauty,' she continues, with a coy flick of her hair, 'and for that trust I shall reward you. To revenge your brother's death, you must travel to Crete, which is an awfully long way away. There, before all else, you must seek out Ariadne, daughter of King Minos, who will aid you in your struggle. She is kind and fair – though nowhere near as fair as I am – and you can trust her. Now I shall take you to Tiryns, and there we shall rest. I have one more vital piece of knowledge to impart to you, but that can wait until we are comfortable.' Seeing that your mind bubbles with unanswered questions, she pats your shoulder reassuringly and gives you a winning smile. 'Relax.' Go to **154**.

67

As the horse gallops past, you grab hold of its golden flowing mane, and jump on to its back. The horse careers wildly up and down the beach, and you are hard put to stay on. Eventually the horse calms, and you feel you have the mastery of it. At this point you look down and see an old man standing at the water's edge, robed in sea-greens and blues. In his hands he bears a trident, wreathed in seaweed.

'Well done,' he congratulates you. 'You have pleased me somewhat. For I am Poseidon, not merely god of the seas, but also master of horses. For your good sense, I will reward you. The seas no longer hold peril for you. Continue on your quest with my blessing, though I am unable to grant you your brother's courage, or the wisdom of your father.' With this, the horse gallops to its master and into the sea, and you are forced to scramble off into the salt water, before you are submerged. You are in favour with Poseidon, if he is not your patron. In any case, have 3 Honour points.

Awed at the appearance of Ocean's lord, you travel on beyond Cenchraea, to Crommyon. Go to **100**.

68

The captain is a small, weather-beaten man, and he readily accepts your proffered coins. 'We sail in two hours,' he says, 'and wait for no man.' You wander along the sea-front, watching the gaily painted vessels offloading their wares from far-flung climes: papyrus from Egypt; corn from the Black Sea; pottery from Crete. It is almost time to return to the ship now, and you rush back through the bustling crowds. As you step on to the boat, you see some of the other passengers offering a prayer to the sea god. The sailors take their positions at the oars. You slump down on an uncomfortable wooden bench, as the ship pulls away from the shore. Despite the earlier crowds there are only a few other passengers. Go to **348**.

69
Take 1 Shame point for failing to defend your mother Aethra's honour. Go to **134**.

70
In the morning you are awakened by a man rushing into the inn with horror etched on his face. The king, he says, is dead, struck down in his prime by treachery, like a sturdy tree felled by the woodsman's axe, who sat beneath its shade as a child. Take 2 Shame points for not preventing this foul deed, and get out of town as quickly as you can. Go to **134**.

71
You offer prayers to Ares, and in a cloud of acrid smoke the god appears before you. 'You have chosen me. Good choice. God of war. Strongest of the gods. None of this complicated liberal wisdom nonsense here. Now, what about you? Oh, yes. Objective: Knossos. Kill the Minotaur. Back here. Off you go. Have some supernatural strength to aid you. Bit out of fashion these days, but the old ways are the best.'

You may add 2 to your natural Might on all of your combat rolls. You start on your way to Athens, where your father is king. Turn to **2**.

72

Slowly you creep up behind the old man, so as not to disturb him. You reach and pull another corner of the curtain aside. If Apollo is your patron go to **521**. Otherwise, go to **56**.

73

It is now early in the afternoon, and the sun is less harsh. The pace of the city has slackened. You pass a shrine dedicated to your patron god, where several people pray. Near by, an old, but hale-hearted beggar stands, appealing for your aid, and blessing the hearts of the great-minded folk who heed his pleas.

Will you go up to the beggar and give him a coin (go to **233**)?

Or will you simply walk on out of Mycenae towards Cleonae (go to **536**)?

74

You make one last attempt to persuade the guard to release you. 'Send a message to the king and queen,' you say. 'They will be able to tell that I am indeed Altheus, and not an impostor.' Turn to **241**.

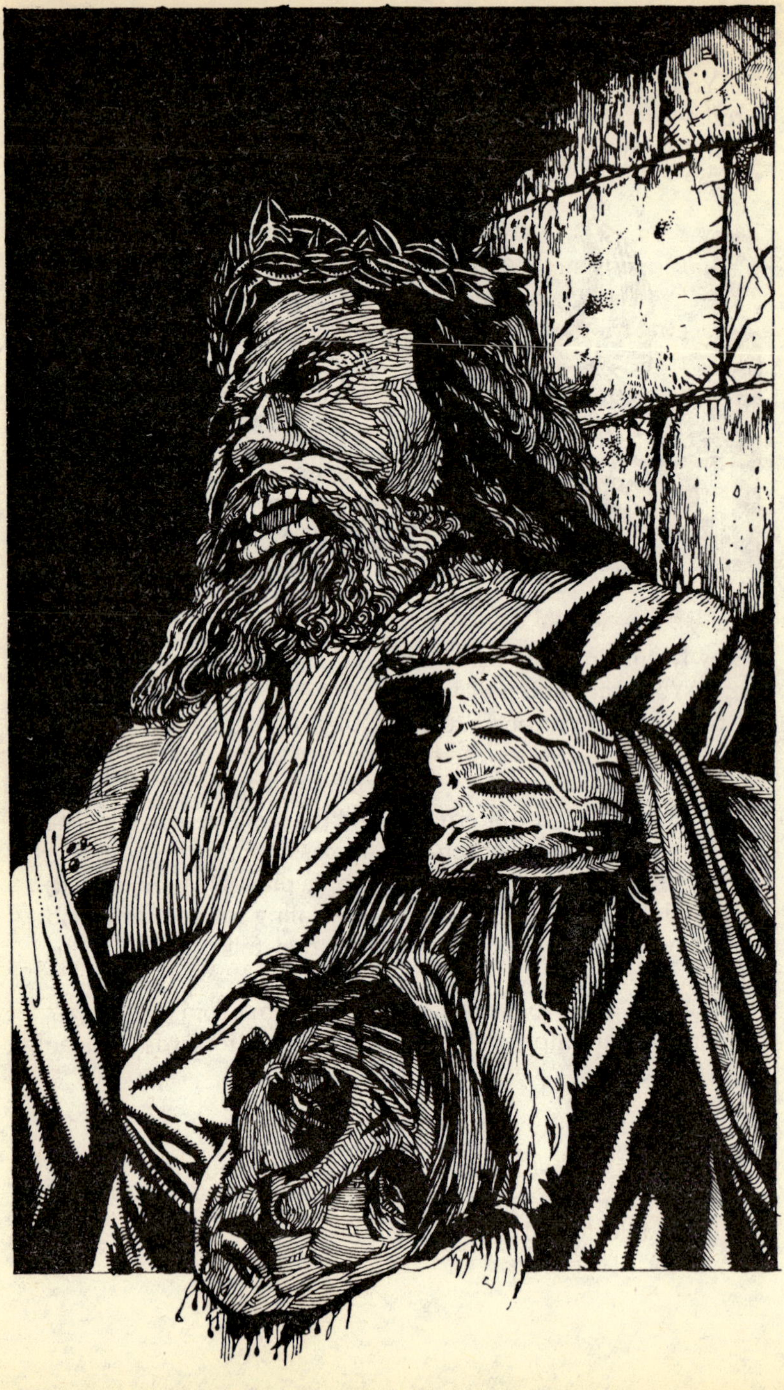

75

Stunned at the attitude of the king towards you, a son of royal house, you hardly resist as you are conducted down to the storeroom. The place is dark and damp, heaped with grain for the city in the coming season. Your sleep that night is troubled by dreams of what fate might await you. Next morning the door opens slowly, and you resign yourself to your end. In rushes the king himself, dripping with blood, and holding the severed head of one of the conspirators.

'You have saved me, my friend,' he roars, 'and I will not forget you. Come, join our feast of celebration.' Go to **310**.

76

You pick her up, and as you lean over to toss the helpless woman into the wild waters, you find you cannot move. Your burden is unbelievably heavy, and you have to set her down at the water's edge. When you look you find that this is no hag, but the immortal wife of Zeus, white-armed Hera.

'Would you treat your mother like this?' she says. 'Would you act like this back in Troezen? No, I don't think you would. You're on your own now, and you won't like it one little bit.' In a blinding flash she has gone.

You must take 2 Shame points. If Hera is your patron, whenever you call on her aid, she will not aid you on a roll of 1–3 on one die, and you lose 2 Honour points. If she is not your patron, you are in Disfavour with her. Go to **294**.

77

The old man is very slow, and he leads you through broad, sunny, well-kept streets, past the temple of Athena, divine protectress of the city. The man, however, now seems to be leading you away from the main thoroughfares of the city, the open meeting-places and the Acropolis.

Eventually the aged beggar stops, and, pointing, cries, 'There, there's your palace. May you have much joy of it.' As you stand, stunned, he laughs hysterically and, with an agility that belies his age, bounds off into a side-street and is gone. Have 1 Shame point for being duped. Go to **334**.

78

Even your mother Aethra's maid would not be turned aside from her task by folk of the lesser sort, peasants who till the soil, or earn their food by the casting of bronze. For you this is indeed shameful. You must take 2 Shame points.

At length the crowd passes you by, and as they do you notice that the object they carry is the corpse of a handsome, dark-haired man, his stomach cut open by the blow of a sword.

You carry on towards the Acropolis. Turn to **230**.

79

Just as you are about to commence your heroic task, you note that branded on each of the cows is a trident, Poseidon's sign. Clearly these are his cattle, and to kill one would invoke his anger. You shout out to your companions, warning them of this danger. Relieved, but without heart-reviving meat, you return to the ship. Go to **595**.

80

No sooner have you grasped the shaft in your hand, than a group of Amazons, a score or more, have surrounded you. It was they who disturbed the night's silence, attracted by your shouts and blows. You explain, nervously, that you are an ambassador of Aegeus, and must see the queen, bearing a token of peace. You are conducted at spear-point to a tent rather larger and grander than the rest. Turn to **8**.

81

Don't be greedy. Lose 2 points of Honour and turn to **263**.

82

'Halt a while, friends,' you say. 'Perhaps you can help me. I know not from where you come, but I must travel far across the wine-dark sea to distant Crete. Perhaps if sun-smitten Naxos, sacred Delos, or gentle Cythera is your home, or some remote isle, then you can tell me of your land.'

The two smile, as if remembering a kindlier place. 'We come from Crete itself,' one of them says, 'land of King Minos. We would gladly return there, but we must first journey to Delphi and Apollo's oracle. If you find yourself in Crete, tell King Minos' daughter that you know of us. My name is Eliduros.' The Cretans make one last gesture of farewell, and then depart out of the gates of Athens on their long journey to Delphi. Go to **394**.

83
Screeching in agony, Tisiphone flies off to the safety of the neighbouring copse. Her sisters follow her, with no stomach for such a fight. 'Yours,' they cry in unison, 'will be the anguish, and yours the mind-killing fear when next you meet the Furies.' With this they ascend aloft into the cool night's air, and are gone. Have 1 Shame point for attacking divinities, but 2 Honour points for your prowess in battle. You are also in Disfavour with the Furies. Go to **501**.

84
Lachesis is one of the three Fates (Moirae). She has two sisters, Clotho and Atropos. Lose 1 Honour point for not knowing. Return to **64**.

85
You fill your goblet, and indeed the wine is excellent. Go to **561**.

86

Eleusis, fairest flower in the Attic garden save only proud Athens herself, home of Demeter's sacred mysteries, bright pearl that gazes over yellow Salamis with kindly eye!

Eleusis, where you, Altheus, now find yourself amid the yearly festival of the corn-goddess, bright-eyed Demeter, fair lady of the earth, and all the fruit it bears.

You move on slowly through the crowds, gathered in awe at the awaited time, when Persephone, spirit of spring, must return to the earth above, and life begin anew. Go to **416**.

87

The guard seems to have heard of a Pyraphas. You have been lucky. But he does not let you in, instead scolding you for using the front entrance. He sends you round the back to a small entrance. From this a smell of cooking drifts, and you can hear the sounds of a feast being prepared.

Do you knock (turn to **7**), or go straight into the kitchen (turn to **270**)?

88

Before any sea voyage you should offer a prayer to Poseidon. If you do offer a prayer, go to **194**. If not, go to **348**.

89

Having extinguished the flame, you turn your attention to the bowl of corn.

Do you eat the corn (**269**)?
Do you burn the corn on the brazier (**404**)?
Do you sprinkle corn on the water (**4**)?
Or do you scatter the corn into the crowd (**32**)?

90

You have been walking along the road for a little while, and at last come upon a road leading deeper into the city. You wish you had asked the guards at the gate the way to the palace. You approach the road, but when you come closer, you see that a large group of people has gathered, apparently stoning two men dressed in strange foreign garb, with double-headed axe motifs sewn into their tunics.

Will you, as a stranger yourself, turn away and carry on (**394**)?

Or will you intervene to save the men from the Athenian mob (**489**)?

91
You may either spend 3 Honour points for Athena's aid, and go to **405**, or lose 1 Honour point and go to **325**.

92
Eventually you come to a pilgrim's hostel, and there, as it is now completely dark, you decide you must stay for the night. You sleep fitfully, and have strange pains in your arms and legs. Many times you think you see your patron, but as you try to speak, the vision disappears. Are the gods trying to tell you something? You can only hope that the oracle has the answer. In the morning you rise, and set off quickly for Delphi, eager to unravel the mystery. Go to **511**.

93
You remember to stop at the shrine and pray to your god. For an instant, you feel the presence of your patron, urging you on to the Cretan shores. Take 1 Honour point for your piety, and return to **73**.

94
People are crowding into a nearby inn. You, too, join in the crush. Water and the smell of damp clothes are everywhere. You warm yourself by the fire. Unable to buy anything to drink, as you have no money left, you have to be content with listening in on the various conversations. Perhaps you will hear something that will be of help to you.

'. . . apparently she was appointed before the other one even left . . .'

'. . . but on the last race they all crashed into each other, and caught fire, and two of them died . . .'

'... apparently the queen makes her own wine. They say it's gorgeous...'

Somebody pushes in front of you to the fire. The rain has now stopped, and slowly the inn empties. You, too, leave and step into the late-afternoon sun. Go to **198**.

95

If ever you are hard pressed in battle, touch this twig with your hand, and it will become a great-shafted spear (Might 6, Protection 0). You may cast it once at your opponent, whereupon it becomes a twig once more, and is thereafter useless. Go to **492**.

96

Eastwards you fare from Athena's town, but your journey is slow, for always you are wary lest the bull take you unawares. You pass through small towns on your way, but take little note of their names as you traverse the gentle rolling uplands – Cephisia, Decelea, Oenoë. At length it is almost dusk, and Marathon is in sight across a flat plain, some half a mile in extent.

Do you go straight into the town, and ask how best the bull might be found and killed (**201**)?

Or do you wait where you are, hoping perhaps to gain a glimpse of the animal (**397**)?

97
As you turn to flee from the combat, you are set upon by a band of Amazons, and taken prisoner. They push you roughly, and take you to a wooden stake in the ground. Here they chain you, taking away all your weapons. You must now wait out the combat, observing, as mere mortals watch helpless, while the gods play out their titanic schemes, heedless of the cries of the toilers below. Go to **150**.

98
You have a serious case of the plague. You are lucky to be alive. You lie for days in a fevered state, cursing the day you crossed the healer god. Your prayers to the Olympians are not answered. At last you are able to rise, but until you reach Athens you will be permanently in a Wounded state (except, of course if you sustain subsequent wounds). As you are about to set out again the goddess Athena appears to you. Go to **213**.

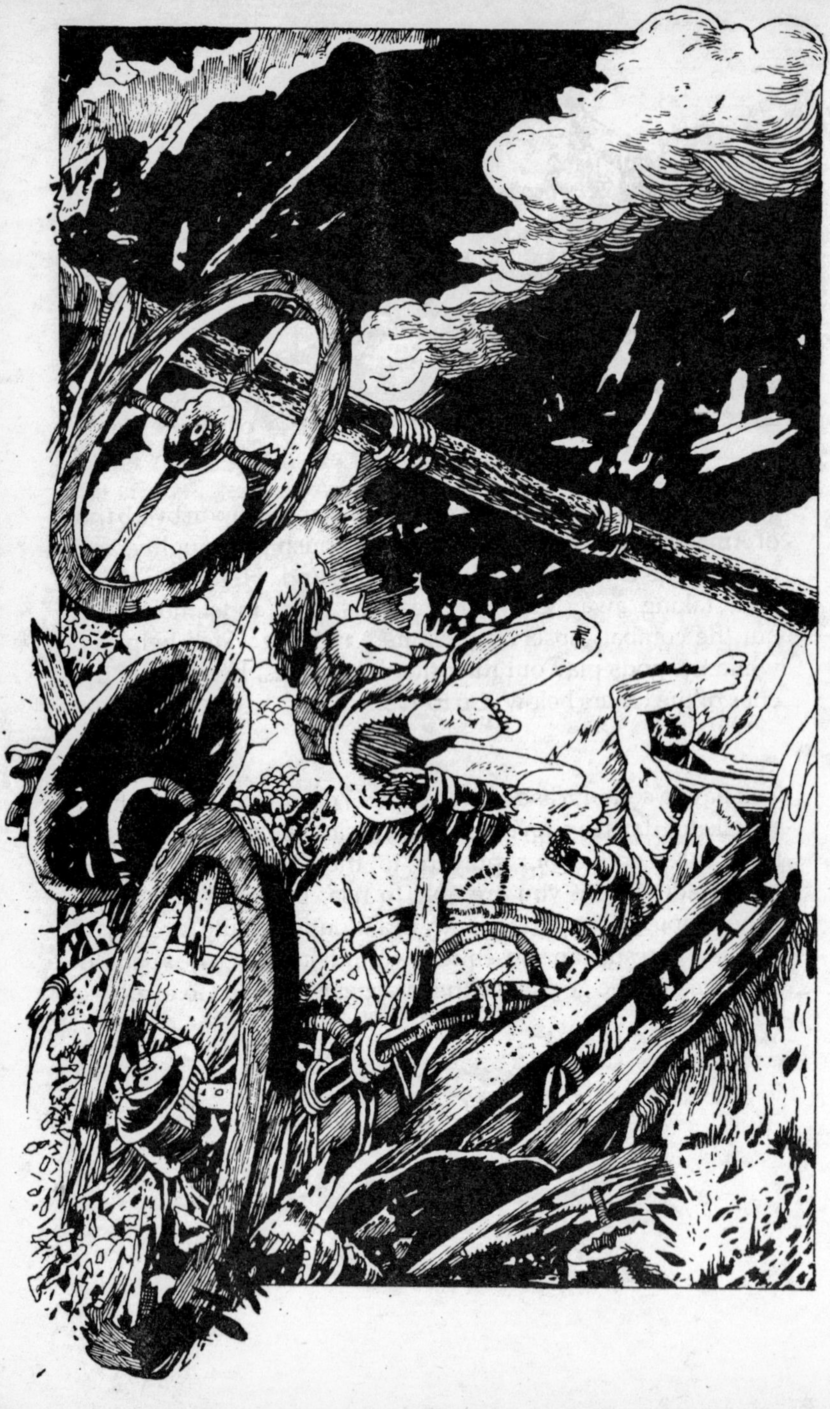

99

The lead chariot loses control, smashes into the wall, and careers on into the crowd. The others, unable to stop in time, slam in behind it, like waves breaking on a sea-shore. Wheels and pieces of splintered wood fly in all directions. Spectators, screaming, stampede everywhere. Several are trampled; others lie dazed and bleeding from the flying fragments. Torches, urns, sticks and cloaks – all are dropped in the panic. Suddenly one of the chariots bursts into flames, ignited by a burning torch. Soon all are ablaze. You clamber unsteadily out of the wreckage, as the flames begin to consume your vehicle. You notice that two drivers are dead. The yellow charioteer has escaped. Some of the citizens make efforts to free the surviving horses, but they are beaten back by the flames.

You stagger away from the chariots on fire. Have 5 Shame points for crashing, and 5 Honour points for survival in the face of such danger.

By the time you reach the inn, the fire has been put out, and you are able to stay safely for the night. In the morning you leave quickly and quietly for Athens (474).

100

Near a small, brightly lit tavern, you see people scattering in all directions, panic and frenzy in their eyes. You try to grab one middle-aged man, but he pushes past, unwilling to stop for anyone. 'The sow!' he warns, as he dashes past. At this cry others join in the headlong flight away from the harbour area. You turn round to see what is the matter, and there, standing, menacing, behind you is a reddy-brown, enormous sow, froth dripping from its lips. It steps towards you, clearly about to charge.

Do you run away as fast as fleet-footed Hermes (go to 493)?

Or do you stand at bay to fight the Crommyonian sow (go to 176)?

101

You tip water on to the grain, creating a brown sludge on the altar. The crowd seem disappointed, and there is some angry shouting. Go to **120**.

102

Now fully armed, you take a moment to pray to your patron before the battle. Then you climb to the top of a high, mud-brick tower at the edge of the walls, to survey the battlefield. The two sides, Athenians and Amazons, are drawn up for the battle, their standards waving in the dawn breeze. For a moment there is silence, like that before the tempest, and then they clash, and it is as when two rivers in winter spate run down from the high hills, and throw together at their meeting the full weight of their water, and far off in the mountains, the shepherds hear the thunder, and stand in awe, wondering at the sound. Such is the shock and clamour from the joining of the battle. You rush down, eager for the fight, and make your way rapidly to the field of war, like a leopard stalking its prey. Soon a small group of Amazons approaches the band of Athenians you have joined, their hair bound with ribbons of gold and silver, their bodies clad in animal skins: they are armed with death-dealing spears.

Do you attack the Amazon wearing the lionskin (**353**), the leopardskin (**124**), or the bearskin (**262**)?

103

As it becomes night you grow more and more tired until you can continue no more. You fall to the ground and collapse into deep, refreshing sleep. Turn to **237**.

104

The man hobbles off and beckons. 'Follow me, I will show you the way to the palace,' he says in answer to your request. Go to **77**.

105

You hand over almost the last of the coins which your mother pressed into your hand as you left the grassy fields of Troezen. You move on towards Cirrha, but for giving in to such shameful threats you must take 1 Shame point. Go to **92**.

106

You make little of these scrolls, save a rhyme telling you to beware lame men, aid sea-serpents, and not to eat beef from Melos. There is a sudden noise, and you must leave before you are discovered, running back in despair to the harbour. Have 1 Shame point, and go to **475**.

107

'Hello, stranger,' coos the rider, evidently a very beautiful woman. 'You've come a long way, and you look worn out. Want a ride? I can offer food and succour. Jump up behind and hold on tight.' If you accept turn to **66**; if you refuse, turn to **135**.

108

'Father!' you cry, realizing with a start that this is the first time you have addressed Aegeus thus. 'There is a way the dark pain of death can be avoided this day, and the horse-haired helmets of the warriors of Athens can be worn proudly, yet those warriors live. For the cause of the enmity between you and the Amazons is a golden hairpin. It is sacred to Hera. To give it up is no great dishonour and Hate's dread wrath could be turned aside. No good can come of keeping it.'

Aegeus thanks you, his son, heartily, for he is war-wearied and has no stomach for the fight with the Amazons. Quickly he scurries off to the treasury and soon returns with the hairpin. 'Go quickly, now,' he says, 'and return this to Antiope, so there may be peace.'

Do you go to the Amazon camp fully armed (**573**)?

Or do you go without any weapons as a token of peace (**367**)?

109

In this part of the city, what houses there are seem much grander. Near one of them a dog is chained, so that it cannot run freely. You approach it tentatively, not knowing how far it can move. Go to **15**.

110

Have 6 Honour points for your victory. You gesture to the bandits, now unarmed, to go down the stairs. The innkeeper sees you, and seems about to say something, but when he notices the bandits he rushes off instead, to serve some of the customers – farmers, drinking lazily in the morning sun before going off to tend their herds and fields. You carry on towards the temple. The road is winding, and on each side groups of trees sway gently in a light breeze. The bandits guide you to within sight of the temple. You admire the tall pillars, still white and unsullied by the passing of Chronos the leveller. A sudden noise startles you from your dreaming. You turn round to see that the bandits have slipped away. There will be no chance of finding them again, you realize. Go to **216**.

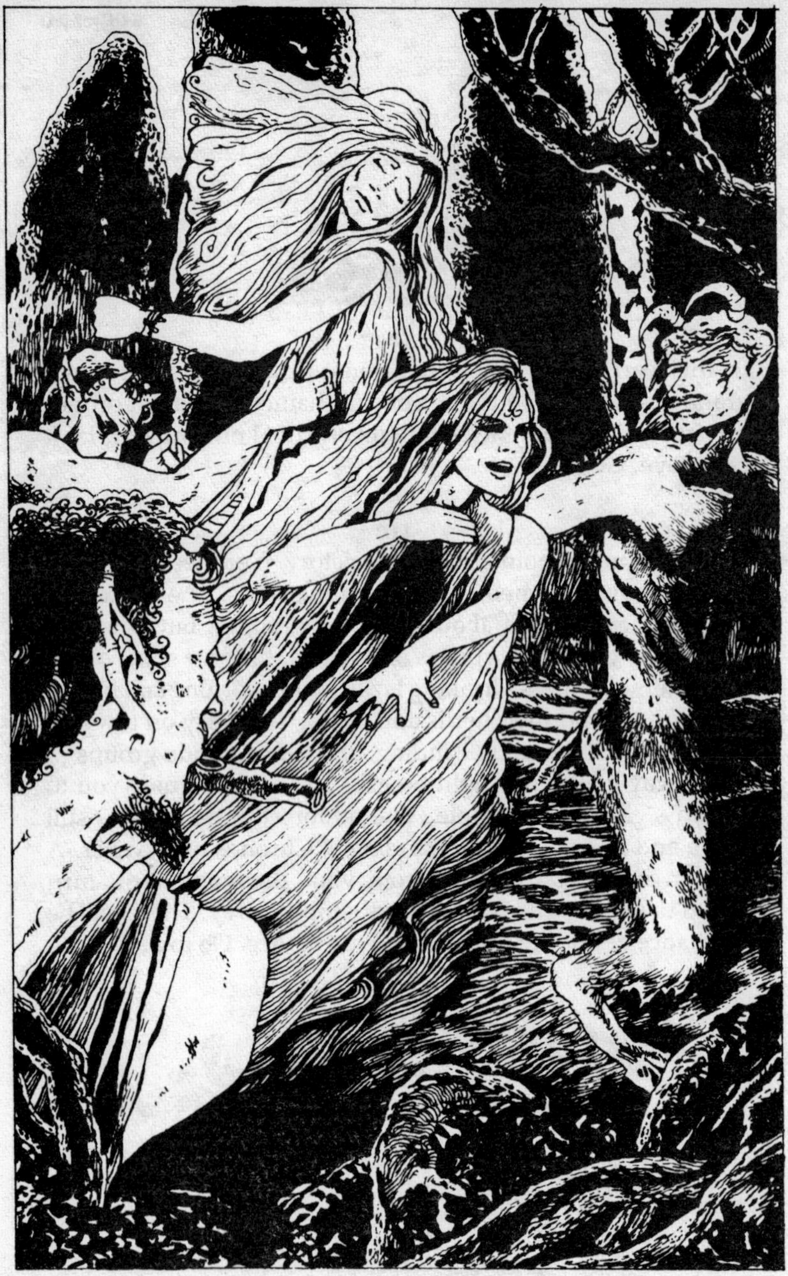

111

After a few minutes you rouse yourself. You are lost, and it is nearing dark. The moon barely penetrates the leafy canopy. From afar you can hear the strains of flutes, and high-pitched giggling. You move cautiously towards the apparent source of the noise. A moonlit clearing opens out in front of you, and you pause at the edge. You gaze in wonder at the scene before you. Nymphs and satyrs frolic in wild abandon. Go to **467**.

112

You are on your way to the Delphic oracle. Try asking there. Have 1 point of Shame, and go to **511**.

113

You may offer him any one of these providing you have it.

The corn-ear brooch (**610**).
The golden cup (**246**).
Your mother's gem (**288**).
The jewelled mirror (**481**).

If you do not possess any of these, or do not wish to risk losing the bet, turn to **9**.

114

Escape is useless: you should have put your trust in the gods. As the life-cloying liquid stifles your breath, you have time to scream a prayer to Zeus, but he will only listen if you have not yet disturbed him. If this is so, go to **144**. If not then Altheus will fight no more bandits!

115

A man, clad in armour, rushes up the steps, elbowing you and pushing you into the mass of pilgrims. You realize that you have been expelled from the temple at Delphi. Lose 2 Honour points. You must depart from Delphi and carry on to Thebes (**191**), picking your weapons up from the place you left them.

116

As you reach a minor crossroads at the start of the town itself, you see a group of men clustering around a low altar. One of them carries a dull iron sickle, another a squealing jet-black puppy. Two of the group hold it down while the officiating priest prepares to strike. The sun casts an elongated shadow, making the men seem from a distance like strange giants.

Do you pass on quickly by (**188**)?

Or do you intervene to save the animal (**576**)?

117

You pray to Poseidon the earth-shaker, and, sure enough, the ground trembles beneath you. As you look up, the waterspout from the fountain forms into the face of an old, white-bearded man. 'So, you're Altheus, are you? Not half the man your father was. Or your brother, come to that. Never mind. Come and pray to me when you have some sailing to do. Until then, kindly leave me alone.'

The ways of the gods are strange. You set out for Athens. Turn to **2**.

118

Zeus the life-bringer appears and touches your severed limbs gently. Overcome by his majesty you faint, and when you awake your terrible wounds are healed. You can walk once more.

'If only,' you think to yourself, 'I had not allowed Sleep to dull my mind, I might have noticed the warnings of the Olympian gods.' Go to **263**.

119

Even badly wounded as they are, the men appear to be unwilling to surrender to you. You turn around to leave the kitchen and see the reason why. Four more guards block your exit. Barring the way into the palace are three more. It is hopeless. You allow yourself to be led off, disarmed and dispirited. Turn to **459**.

120

The priestess steps forwards and speaks once more: 'Citizens, this is not one of us, but a stranger. He cannot be expected to know the proper conduct of our rites. Stranger, be on your way,' she says, not unkindly. As you hurry away, you see the priestess choose another to participate in the Eleusinian worship. Go to **138**.

121

Have 1 Shame Point for surrendering. The man, however, shows no mercy, and terror racks your ruined body as his sword comes down to sever life from your limbs. You have failed Apollo, and from Zeus there will come no aid.

122

By the light of the approaching stranger's lamp, you see to your horror that on the table are the documents penned by your noble father Aegeus to Minos of Crete. The captain must have done this, while his brain was fuddled by wine. You gather them up and rush out of the door. For a second you confront the grim-faced innkeeper, but you do not stop at his amazement, running off down the dark streets to the harbour. Have 1 Shame Point, and go to **575**.

123

The doorway leads to a large, but bare room. Beyond this is a tiny study, closed off by silken hangings. Here your father draws up the edicts of his rule, or, more often, has scribes do it for him; but this is a private document. Go to **155**.

124

The Amazon who wears the leopardskin has Might 8, Protection 15.

If you die and are saved by Zeus, go to **572**.
If you retreat, go to **97**.
If you surrender, go to **376**.
If you Seriously Wound the Amazon, go to **366**.

125

Roll a die. You may expend this number of Honour points in a prayer to Poseidon, and go to **424**. Otherwise, you face the churning sea without a prayer to the ocean god. Go to **257**.

126
The priest motions to two burly acolytes, who walk slowly towards you, clearly about to expel you from Apollo's shrine. Not wishing to desecrate the temple with blood, you stride boldly through the doors, pick up your weapons and are away, down the road to Thebes (go to **191**).

127
The innkeeper, still terrified even though you have surrendered, simply pushes you out of the inn, without tending to your torn skin, and blocks up the doorway where triple-layered pine once stood. Go to **23**.

128
Taking the sacred hairpin in your hands, you set off for the Amazon camp. Swiftly you realize that to go unannounced would be to suffer the fate of a man who walks into the den of the lion which cannot hunt, for it has a thorn in its paw: he is devoured by the very beast he would have saved. You hold the great pin out in front of you; it is large, almost the size of a sword. Those Amazons who see you dare not slay you, for to do so would be to desecrate their land's most sacred relic. Instead, they guide your way to the tent of the queen, man-slaying spears barring your way elsewhere. Go to **8**.

129
Do you fear dogs? Do you think one would dare to bite a hero? Lose 1 Honour point. Go to **15**.

130
You could pick up their knives (Might 2), if you wished. Now return to **110**.

131
You could step out and seek the hospitality of these woodland creatures (**10**), or you could press on into the night, in the hope of getting to Thebes (**616**).

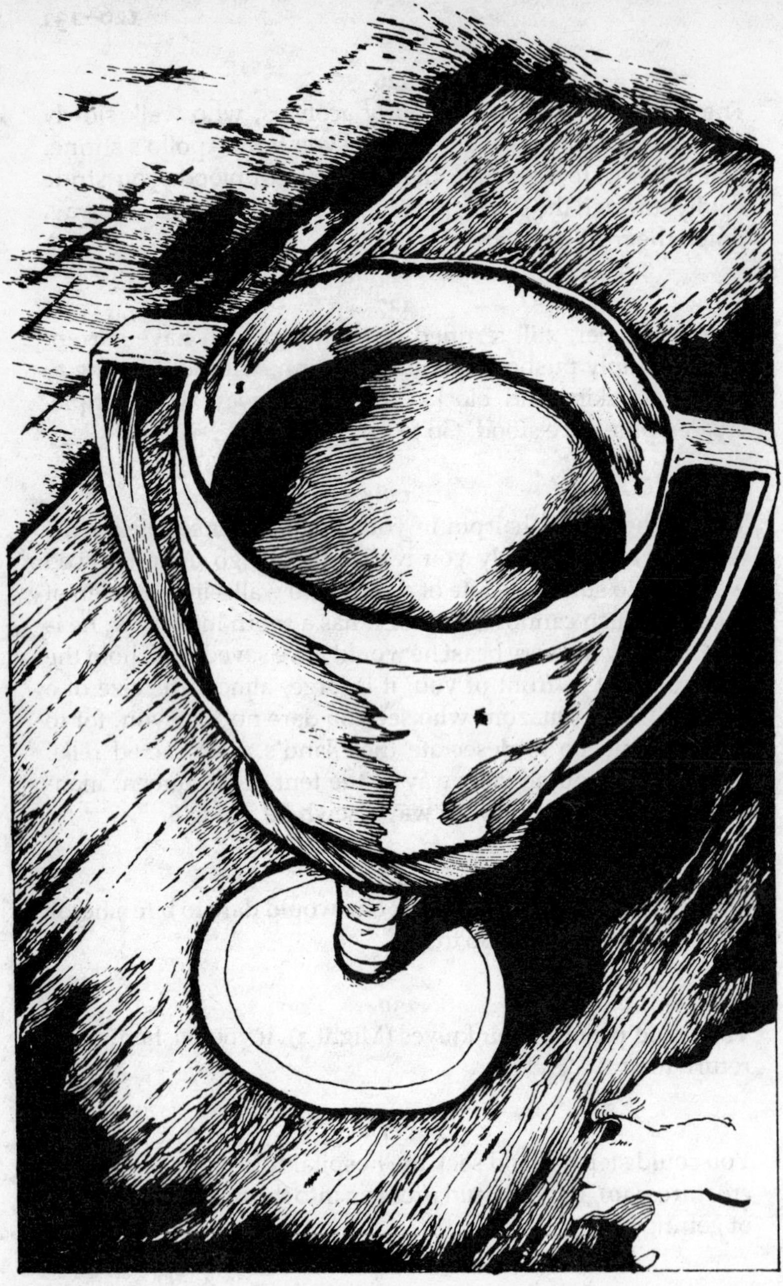

132

You drain the goblet quickly, but notice a bitter after-taste. You begin to choke, and soon find you cannot breathe. The wine is poisoned! You gasp out one last time, before you can breathe no more. Your travels are over, and to the end of time you will dwell, a pitiful shade in Hades, unless you can pray to Zeus. If so, you recover after a time, and find yourself still at the table with a crowd gathered around you. The queen is gone. Turn to **170**.

133

No sooner has the bright-eyed goddess gone than she is back, this time without the girl. 'Silly me,' she whimpers. 'Immortality makes one so forgetful. I'm sure there's something I've got to tell you. Oh! That darling child Ariadne. No, that wasn't it.' The goddess's radiant brow creases and she begins to frown. 'Never mind!' She flicks her hair back and turns to go. She puts her hand to her mouth and laughs sweetly. 'That was it!'

'What was it?' you ask.

She pouts. 'Ask me nicely or I shan't tell you,' she breathes.

Tired, but no wiser, you leave Megara, and carry on down the road to Eleusis, marvelling at the ways of the white-armed one. Go to **86**.

134

With thankfulness in your heart you quit the city of Thebes. You carry on up the road, passed by farmers with their bullock-carts slowly making their way to Acharnae. The path is cracked and rutted and the fields to either side are flooded by the spring-swollen streams. A fallen tree blocks the way for a while but you quickly clamber over it. You soon reach the foothills of the range before Acharnae. The going is hard, but there is no snow. As you climb, the wind grows colder and you shiver slightly. Soon, however, you are over, and you come to the outskirts of Acharnae, barely visible in the dusk. Go to **116**.

135

'Ah, foolish youth,' she chides, 'I am Aphrodite, your chosen goddess.' With these words she is revealed in shining radiance. 'Don't be so shy, silly. Redeem yourself by travelling to Crete.' She runs her hand through her hair and preens a bit, and then turns back to you. 'There you will find a maiden called Ariadne. Rescue her. Now off to Athens and your father's house. Remember that I am your patron: you must cherish beauty, for one day it may save you.' It is getting dark and you can see no lights ahead. If you decide to bed down beside the road, turn to **237**; if you decide to press on regardless, turn to **103**.

136

The bull has Might 10, Protection 18.
  If you defeat it, turn to **282**.
  If you retreat, turn to **515**.
  If you die, but are saved by Zeus, turn to **335**.

137

Still musing on the song of the bard, you press on briskly. Soon the street divides. Do you turn left into a street of poor dwellings (**394**), or right to an area where there are few houses (**109**)?

138

As you leave Eleusis behind, the way is lined on either side by olive trees, and some distance from the town a track joins the main path to your left. You pause a while in the hope that some traveller will be able to tell you the road to take, but no one comes. Impatiently, you decide to move on.
  Do you take the track (**531**)?
  Or do you carry on down the road (**474**)?

139

The spear-armed warrior looks exactly like your patron Ares. Turn to **543**.

140

As the evening wears on you realize that the wine is somewhat stronger than it should be. You try to get up, but find you cannot move. The conversation now sounds far off, and in a while you lapse from awareness. Go to **560**.

141

You manoeuvre the boat away from the rocks. The woman throws her arms round your neck and kisses you on the forehead. Just as you are beginning to enjoy yourself, the husky-voiced one disappears, and you are left to swim back to the ship. Have 3 Honour points. Go to **608**.

142

At long last you reach the Piraeus, the well-built harbour of Athens. A host of people are assembled there, busily loading and unloading goods from the islands. Your ship is obvious: a great but weather-beaten pine vessel with sails of deep black, draped in cloths of black, its crew dressed in sombre robes.

A small man in a white-trimmed cloak beckons to you. He is the captain, and they have delayed sailing for you. They must leave within minutes, or the tide will prevent them for another twelve hours. You rush aboard and are shown below decks to a large room where the crew sleep and keep their possessions. Here you stow your weapons, and go to join the captain. Go to **327**.

143

Through the hail of stones and rocks you rush, not fearful for your life. You reach the place where the man stands, but find nothing. The warrior is gone, and the rockfall has ceased. Somehow you have been tricked, and your mind is seized by confusion. Only the lame man is left, and he seems angry.

'Ares you have saved, and not Hephaestus. Perhaps you sought to preserve the spear, and so I will not punish you. Yet you must always aid the lame and crippled, Altheus, or it will be to me you answer.' With this the god seems to walk into the base of the black rock cliff, and is gone. Go to **495**.

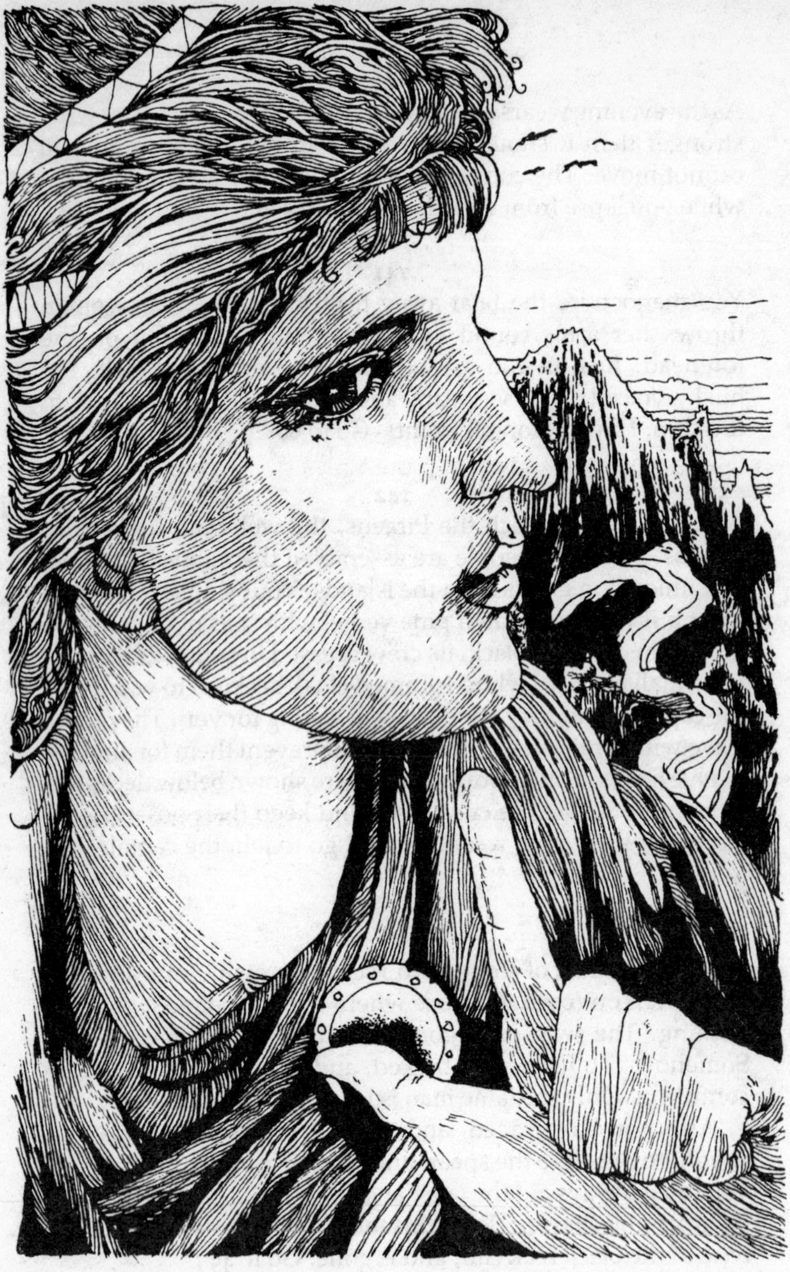

144
You find yourself lying beside the fountain, gasping for air, stripped of all your arms and armour. Quickly you gather your wits, and leave the temple before the two men return. Stumbling and falling, you rush you know not where. Go to **536**.

145
Although you have automatically succeeded in escaping, you must take 1 Shame point, and you are now in Disfavour with Asclepius. Go to **536**.

146
'Go to the Cretan labyrinth,' the queen of the gods continues, 'taking care to keep your armour bright. Don't upset King Minos, and try not to be too brutal to the poor Minotaur. Take plenty of rest, and keep away from the slut Ariadne. Now what you do is this. Find the centre of the labyrinth, and there you should see your brother. He's dead, of course. Anyway, he had a sword; he left it lying around when he died. It's just getting rusty, so I thought it might make a nice ornament for the lesser gods to admire. In any case it was I who gave it to Aegeus in the first place, so it's only fair. Now hurry along, and do stop standing in that absurd river.' So the goddess speaks, and then is gone, to see that Zeus is keeping things in order. Go to **294**.

147
You rush down past the puppy and statue into the darkness of a tunnel. You find it harder and harder to push forward. Wind and dust blow into your eyes and you are forced to close them. At last you reach the end. Go to **585**.

148
You leave the temple steps far behind you, and wonder what would have happened had you saved the maiden. For your rejection of beauty you are in Aphrodite's Disfavour. You carry on out of the town, moving slowly towards Eleusis. Go to **86**.

149

The man is amazed that you have surrendered to him. 'I can see you are a sensible man,' he says. 'Come with me and join our band.'

Do you take up his offer (go to **522**), or do you leave the market and Megara, and set off for Eleusis (go to **86**)?

150

You must have fallen asleep, for when you awake, you are surrounded by a group of armed warriors. This must be your end. When you open your eyes again, however, you see that they are in fact Athenians. Seeing that you are Altheus, they send for a blacksmith, who soon frees you. It is evident that the Athenians have won, and as the silver-robed moon begins her long ascent, and dark Night her dominion on the earth, you make your way back to Aegeus' palace. You must, however, have 2 Shame points for being captured and humiliated by your opponents. Go to **441**.

151

With horror, the Athenians see that they have attacked a hero. Not waiting for their women, they run off into the streets, and attempt to take refuge in a nearby tavern. Their companions join them, and at length the young woman, whose husband is clearly the one whose funeral this was to have been, gives you a last look of hatred, and then she, too, takes off.

For your victory you may only have 3 Honour points, won as it was against such feeble foes. You now carry on towards the Acropolis. Turn to **230**.

152

Down towards the metropolis you trek, the hill paths, littered with rubble, forcing you to tread warily. Shepherds graze their sheep to the left and right, and as you come closer to the city, carts begin to pass you, plying between Corinth and its sister port Cenchraea. Go to **211**.

153

'Fool!' cries Alecto as you fall to your knees, 'to pick a fight with the Furies! Now we cannot harm you, but soon there will be no place on earth where you can hide from our vengeance, and you will wish that your mother had never borne you.' Take 1 Shame point, in addition to the normal 1 point for surrendering, and carry on in the knowledge that you are in Disfavour with the Furies. Go to **167**.

154

The goddess's horse is fast, and you soon arrive in Tiryns. You see an inn with a gaily painted wooden sign, 'The house of Procrustes'. The goddess shakes her head. 'I have my own little place, close by. It's far cosier.'

You ride through the dark streets to a secluded mansion. Even the porch is larger than the cottage in which you have lived all your life, and priceless blue glass statuettes stand all around in alcoves.

'They're of me,' breathes the goddess. 'Rather nice, don't you think? This one's terribly good, but the arms are missing.' You go inside, and sit down. You ask about the vital piece of knowledge which the goddess has not told you.

'Later,' whispers Aphrodite. Turn to **223**.

155

The king seats himself at the table and speaks once more. 'Altheus,' he says, 'there are things I must say to you that I could not say before the nobles of the city and visitors from afar. Minos is an implacable man, and I fear he may not accept our offer of tribute. Were the Minotaur to be killed, however, he might see the wisdom of an alternative course, or even be too weakened to attack Athens again, for it is said that the presence of the beast in Crete gives divine strength to their armies. I will give the captain of the ship which bears you instructions to journey under a black sail. If you succeed, change them to white, and I will know at your coming that you have succeeded. Be swift, for already discontent grows daily at the sacrifices, and my guards have dispatched five men to the care of black-hearted Hades. Yet before you go, there is one service more I must ask of you. The Amazons, women-warriors, are marching to our city to besiege it. No one can divine the reason why, not even the seer Honis. We need your aid to fight off this threat.'

With this, Aegeus starts to write the letters for the Cretan king. When he has finished, he seals them with hot wax and hands them to you.

Do you thank Aegeus, and depart to your bed-chamber, to await the attack next morning (**52**)?

Or do you decide to stay awake, lest the attack come at night (**497**)?

156

'You have betwayed your patwon's twust,' continues the fair-faced goddess, 'and you must pay the pwice. To wedeem yourself you must continue without my aid until you weach Athens. Farewell.' With this, the queen of owls returns to high Olympus, and leaves the lands of mortals far behind. Until you reach Athens, you gain no bonus to your Protection in combat, and must pay the full price in Honour when you take a non-existent hint. Carry on your way down the road to **51**.

157

In a flash of blinding light Ares the strong-armed bars your way from the room. 'Stop, Altheus,' he booms. 'Discipline. First warning. Last warning. Go to it. No shirking. No retreat. No surrender.' He disappears.

Warned by your patron, you must attack or take 3 Shame points. Your opponents, startled by the war-bringer's appearance, have not yet attacked.

If you attack, go to **333**.

If not, go to **228**.

158

It is now just before noon. High overhead, the sun seems to set the very sea aflame. The ship is coming closer to the Cretan land. At the very edge of the horizon one of the Athenian girls thinks she can make out the shoreline.

If Aphrodite is your patron go to **471**.
Otherwise go to **28**.

159

The lion-robed woman drops her spear and begs for mercy. She can take no more of the fight. Near by you can hear clanking and rattling noises.

Do you kill the Amazon, and make your way onwards (**252**)?

Or do you permit her to live, simply divesting her of the sharp-tipped spear, which has Might 2 (go to **80**)?

Whatever you decide to do, you may have 4 Honour points for your victory.

160

The bull is a particularly fearsome creature, so, for the duration of this combat only, your Might is reduced by 1 point. Turn to **136**.

161

You reach Megara by midday. The fresh sea-breeze of the coast road blows your hair, which waves as do the golden ears of corn under the summer sun, before the farmers come to harvest them with their sickles of shining metal, laughing and warming to the task. You could go to the famous market at Megara (go to **470**), or alternatively simply wander about the town for a few hours (go to **539**).

162

You are now out of range of Talos' boulders, and can sail towards Crete. As you make for the coast, you see that the bronze giant has caught a foot on the sea-bed and fallen over. Go to **384**.

163
As the second strong-greaved foeman falls, you see the fountain flowing in healing water once more, clear and sparkling with the god's favour. The face of the statue, no longer twisted, smiles and seems to look at you in thanks. You are clearly now a Favoured one of Asclepius (note this on your Chronicle Sheet). You may also have 6 Honour points for your victory in combat. Go to **536**.

164
The guard looks at you blankly. He has clearly not heard of anyone named Styrikon. Seizing advantage of his momentary hesitation, you push forward, trying to gain access to the palace. He, however, calls for help, and soon two more heavily armed guards bar your way with swords.

Do you attack them (**226**)?

Or do you submit to being arrested (**459**)?

165
Away from the Amazon camp you flee, as if the very Furies were on your tail, screaming for your blood, and tearing your flesh with their claws. You reach Athens in minutes, and while the king stands, gravely considering events, you describe your reception. War is now inevitable, and it is you, Altheus, who have failed to stop it: grim Death's cup will soon be overflowing. Take 1 Shame point. You prepare for battle. Go to **102**.

166
The guards gaze at you astounded, for they thought you were dead. They do not make any effort to bind your wounds; they strip you of your armour, and drag you away down into the depths of the palace. Go to **459**.

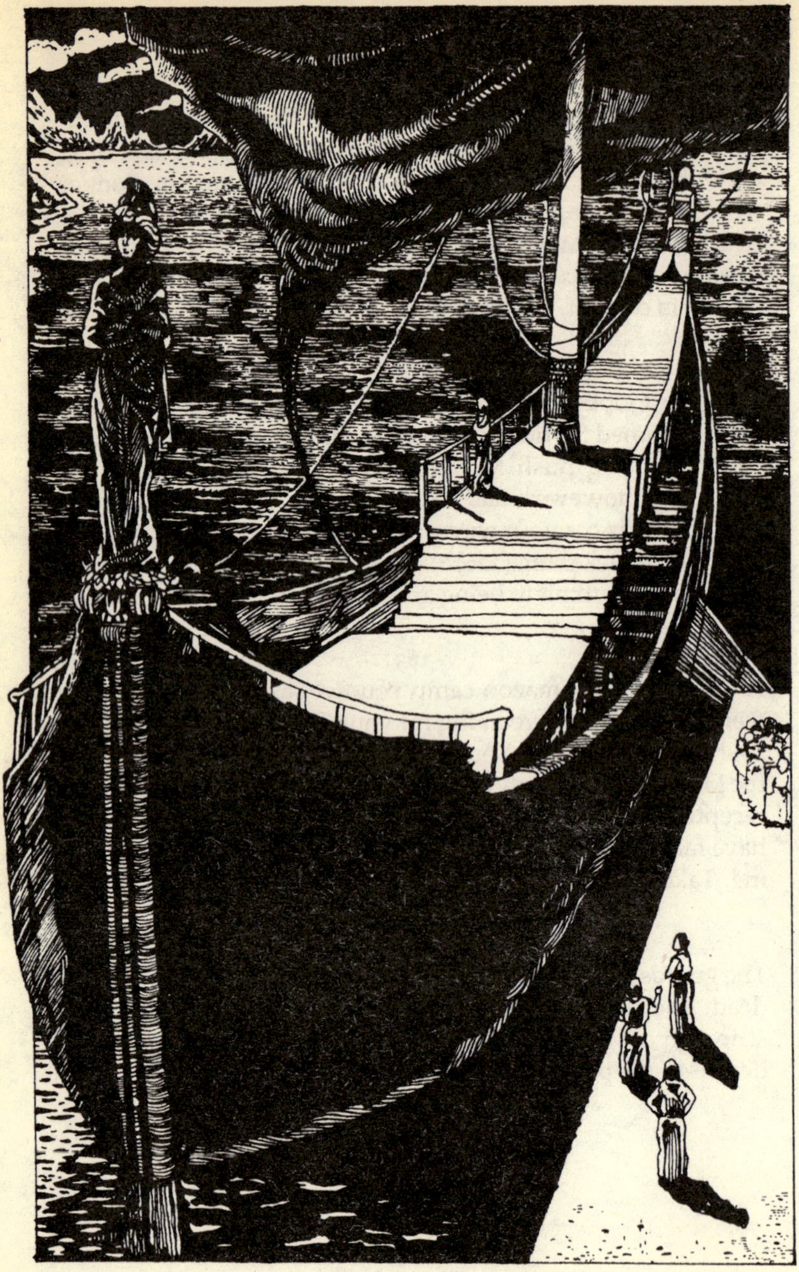

167

To Piraeus of the great-carved ships you come, and there at the harbour's edge stands the boat that will take you to Crete and the well-founded citadel of Knossos: a great, pine-built vessel, sails of cloth deep-dyed in black, rowing-benches wreathed in black, oars painted black while the crew wear robes the colour of the night. Yet the ship is old, its hull encrusted with the debris of the seas. The figurehead of Athena at the prow, once the proud harbinger of an Athenian crew, is now faded and saddened by the cargo it carries. In a huddle stand the fourteen young men and women destined for death in the Cretan labyrinth. You approach a small, brown-bearded man, whose robe is trimmed with white, standing on the quayside. He is indeed the captain, but says that the ship cannot sail tonight as the tide is wrong. Your hurried journey from Athens was unnecessary: you could have avoided the Furies! You retire below decks, and there sleep in the cabin where the crew have their quarters.

In the morning you awaken refreshed, and go back to the deck, where Dawn has already brought her message of light to the realms of earth. Go to 327.

168

In the temple at Troezen, you bow down at the statue of Athena and pray. The room grows quiet and peaceful. Then, in a shimmering haze, the statue stirs into life.

'Altheus, son of Aegeus, you have chosen wisely, and wisely shall I aid you in your quest. In weturn, I ask of you one favour. Go to Cwete and wecover your bwother's body, that it may be buwied in Athens with fitting wites. Good luck.' Athena is goddess of defensive war, so you may add 1 to your Protection value. In addition, you need pay no Honour when instructed to do so, if you take a look twenty numbers on and there is no hint. If the penalty is in Shame, you must still take it.

The statue falls silent, and will speak no more. You set out for Athens, where your father is king. Turn to 2.

169

This time you are driving in the race. The rules are as before, except that you are the new number 2 (the red team). The race is now two laps of the wall perimeter (twenty points). As before, if your patron is Poseidon, a roll of 5 will advance you one space, and if you are in Favour with Poseidon, a roll of 5 will advance you one space if you expend 1 Honour point for it. If you are in Disfavour with Poseidon, you do not advance on a roll of 6, but all the other chariots do.

If you are clear how to conduct the race, do so and turn to the end of this paragraph. Otherwise, here is a summary of the rules.

Roll two dice. If they are both 6, a crash has occurred. Roll a further die. If it is 1, 2, 3 or 4, that numbered chariot has crashed, and is removed from the race. If it is 5, there was a near miss and nobody crashes. If it is 6, all the chariots crash.

If the two dice come up anything other than double 6, each roll between 1 and 4 advances that chariot one space. If 6 is rolled, all chariots advance one space, and if 5 is rolled, none of them do, except for Poseidon's alterations detailed above.

Continue rolling dice, two at a time, until one chariot has moved twenty spaces or until all chariots have crashed.

If you win the race, turn to **14**.

If you lose the race, turn to **271**.

If you crash, turn to **321**.

If all the chariots crash, turn to **99**.

170

The king stares you straight in the face, his gaze like that of the snake-haired Gorgon, freezing you where you stand, his white locks like the snow that lies atop Olympus.

'Who are you, stranger,' he says, his voice strangely rich, and flowing, 'who come to my house thus, and cause such a disturbance? Speak now, and speak the truth, for Zeus protects all strangers, and we mean you no harm.'

Do you hesitate, and wait for the king your father to speak again (**389**)?

Or do you reply 'Altheus' at once (**546**)?

171

The two men drop their daggers and fall to the floor, grasping your feet in a position of supplication.

'Spare us,' they beg, 'and we will lead you to the temple by a safe route.'

Do you accept their offer (go to **110**)?

Or do you kill them anyway (go to **403**)?

172

No need to tread that warily! Lose 1 Honour point, and go on to **211**.

173

You can make little out in the deathly gloom, and you dare not light a lamp. Only snatches of the document emerge.

'. . . Ceos, inhabited by sea-monsters . . .'

'. . . the punishment of those who desecrate Melos . . .'

'. . . on Theros, help the lame man at your peril . . .'

Suddenly you hear a noise. Perhaps someone is coming. Strong fear grips your shoulders.

Do you examine the other table (**122**)?

Or do you leave for the harbour at once (**326**)?

Whichever you decide, you must take 1 Shame point for what you have done.

174

Into the water you plunge, your body shattered by the strong arm of Talos. Perhaps the Cretan quest, your swordquest, was hopeless, you muse, as your life-spirit seeps from your body; but it is not the way of the hero to sit at home and die old, the challenges unfaced.

175

You decide that it would be wise to scout the Amazon camp, now close to the walls of Athens itself, for you may discover the reason for the attack.

Silently you pass through the city and out of the gates, the guards saluting as you pass. You can soon see the campfires of

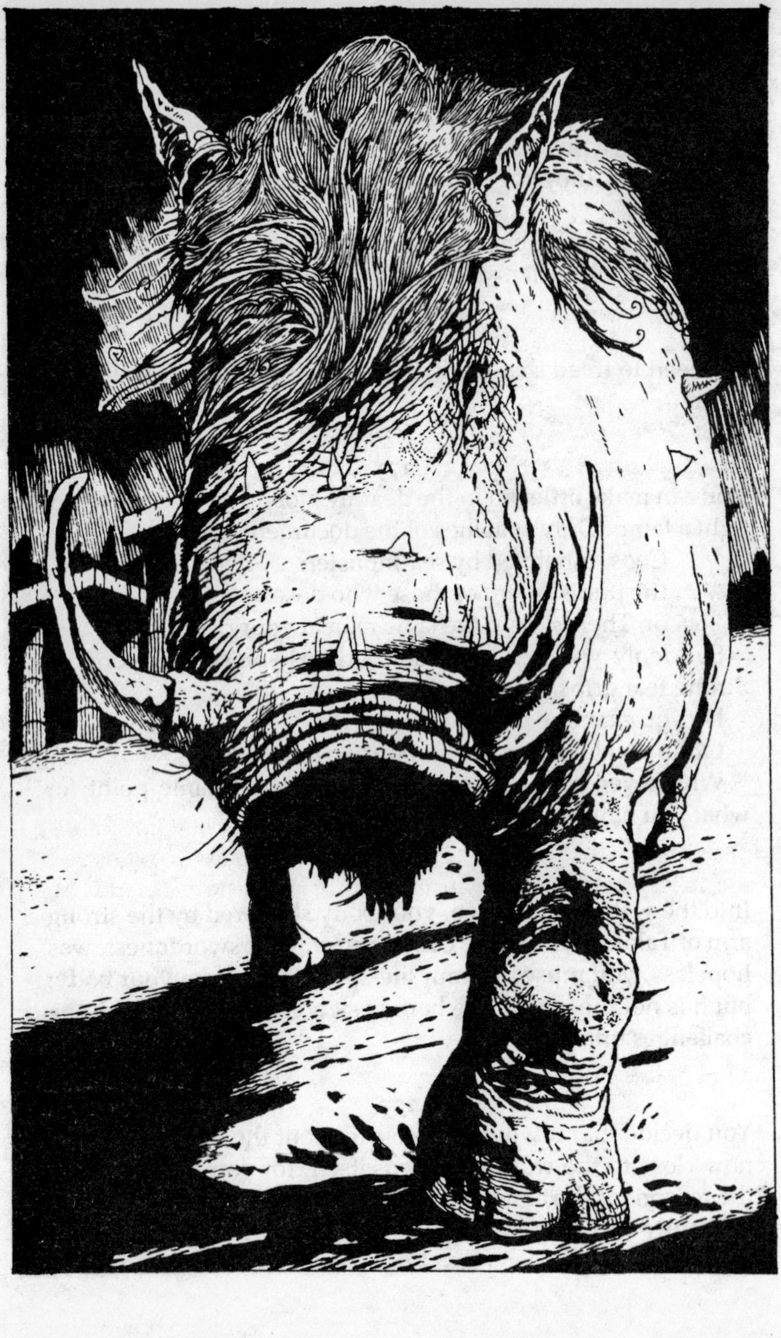

the Amazons, lighting up the midnight sky, as the shepherd's burning cottage illuminates the tiny valley, driving off both sheep and the neighbours who had come to help, fearful now of the fate in store for them.

Go to **222**.

176

The sow (Might 12, Protection 6) charges you.
If you defeat it, go to **615**.
If you successfully retreat, go to **493**.
If you die, but are saved by Zeus, go to **378**.

177

Have 2 Shame points for your brutal and shameful act. Go to **415**.

178

Talos is nowhere to be seen, and you realize that he must come upon you from the west, so that to move into the shore with an easterly slant would give you a better chance of avoiding him. Just as you confide your heaven-sent insight to the captain, the earth beneath the sea begins to tremble. The very fish in their seaweed-covered realm can feel the shock. Talos comes! You look to the west and there, towering above the cliffs, is Talos, perhaps two hundred feet tall. Yet he is too far away to destroy the ship with his brazen arms. Instead he casts rocks at you. There will be time for five rounds of combat, and the only weapons you have which will reach that far are a supply of the captain's harpoons (Might 2, Protection 0).

Talos is Might (*)14, Protection 18, and the rocks are counted as Might 0.

If you hit Talos three times, go to **464**.
If you retreat, go to **549**.
If you surrender, go to **443**.
If you die, go to **174**.
After five rounds of combat, go to **162**.

179

The monster is Might 22, Protection 14.

If you attack the creature, turn to **533**.

If you wait, and hope that the creature will not attack, turn to **562**.

180

As the fatal blow is about to be struck, divine Zeus stays the Amazon's spear and takes you, badly injured, to gentle Cythera. Here he heals your wounds, and without a word whisks you back to the battlefield. You must fight on. Return to **102** and choose a different opponent.

181

A low moaning noise issues from behind the curtain. The Pythian priestess has begun to utter the words of Apollo. You notice that a small withered man, dressed in a rich tunic, has pulled aside a corner of the curtain, and seems to be looking at what lies behind.

Do you investigate and look behind the curtain (**72**)?

Do you take no action at all (**442**)?

Or do you pull him away (**284**)?

182

A number of actions spring to mind.

You could eat from the bowl of corn (**269**).

You could burn the corn on the brazier (**404**).

You could sprinkle some corn on the water (**4**).

Or you could scatter the corn into the crowd (**19**).

183

You should drink from the fountain of the healer god. If you do drink, then for the next combat only, the god will aid you. Instead of being Wounded when an opponent hits you in combat the first time, you will remain Healthy. Only the second hit will move you to Wounded, and so on. Go to **536** to continue your journey.

184
Have 4 Shame points (2 'extra' Shame points) for your horrific act, unworthy indeed of a true hero. Go to **415**.

185
You sit, depressed, in the cell for what seems like hours. You do not know when you will be released, or indeed whether you will be released at all. At length a maidservant comes and leaves some bread and a pot filled with water. Eagerly, you eat the meagre fare, and pray to the gods for your release.

If Aphrodite is your patron and you desire her help, turn to **491**.

Otherwise, turn to **54**.

186
Bedraggled and thoroughly miserable, you press on through the city until you reach a crossroads. You hardly notice that the rain has ceased, and it is only when the sun peers tentatively through the threatening clouds that you begin to smile, once more amicable Altheus. Go to **198**.

187
The healer god, in repayment for your earlier service, lights up the barn with a healing glow. The rats, harbingers of death and disease, cannot bear the touch of Asclepius, and they perish, withered where they stood, as the golden ears of corn die at the scorching touch of Skiron, the wind of the north-west. Your task is done, and the town of Pagae is set free from the plague. You are in favour with Athena, if she was not your patron. In any case, you may have 4 Honour points. The lord of the town, seeing what has happened, greets you, but hurries you out of the town, with only a loaf, afraid of the works you might perform in his domain. Go to **51**.

188
The town of Acharnae is in festival at this time of the year, for the annual chariot races are being held this week. All over the

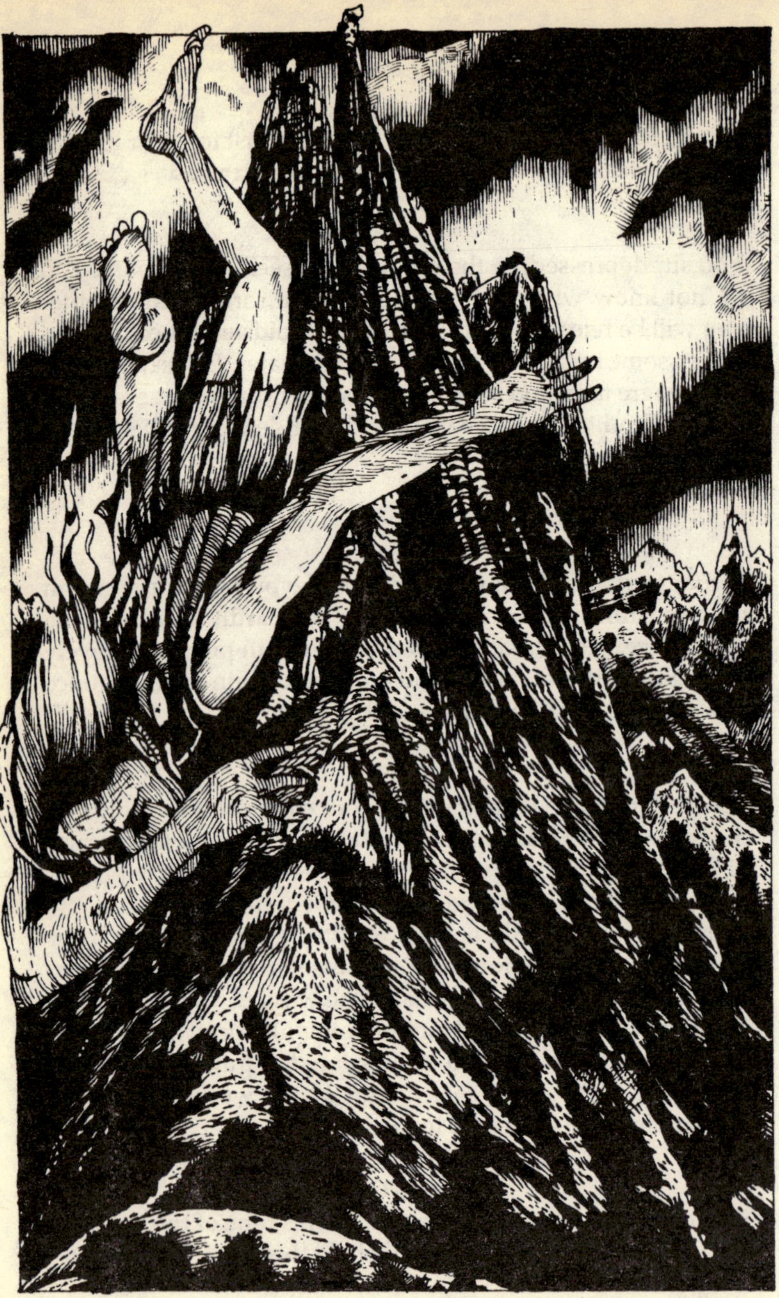

town men prepare their horses and repair their chariots. You have been walking for some time, and so decide to find an inn to rest for a while. You are directed to a small, low building, fringed by trees, where many of the competitors are staying. The price for a night is high, but you can just afford it. The excited chattering of the guests is like the buzz of bees greedy for honey, but you can make out some of it. There is in fact to be a race within the hour around the narrow streets of the town.

Do you go to bed (**513**)?
Or do you set out for the chariot races (**423**)?

189
Pressing on out of the city with a sigh of relief, you walk ahead quickly. A farmer comes up behind you, and offers you a ride in his cart, carrying goat's cheese to the port at Crommyon. The journey is long, and you begin to feel drowsy. You also feel hungry, but it does not look as though the farmer is going to stop to eat.

You could take some of the cheese, without asking the farmer (go to **555**), or you could bide your time (go to **268**).

190
Do you still have your mother's gem? If you do, turn to **505**. If not, turn to **389**.

191
As you walk down the hillside from the temple of the god, an unearthly cry freezes your blood. You look up, startled. From the high crag above a man plummets, like the eagle's egg, dislodged from the lofty eyrie, falls, and its life's majesty is done before it starts.

You stand in silence for a moment, wondering at the fate of the dead man, and then carry on towards Thebes (go to **392**).

192

Inspired by warlike Ares the man-slaughterer, god of battle, you break down the solid pine door with your bare hands. The wood splinters, as does the bark of the ship torn open by the jagged rocks, its sailors crying out in despair, while the earth-shaker, Poseidon, hears them not; so does the innkeeper scream out, and you pay him no heed.

You wound him at once, and the blood flows free from a gash in his side. He grabs a stick from a table and goes into the attack.

The innkeeper has Might 3, Protection 10, but the stick is Might 1, making Might 4 in all:
If you retreat, go to **304**.
If you surrender, go to **127**.
If he is Seriously Wounded, go to **401**.
If you die and are saved by Zeus, go to **23**.

193

You feel refreshed, and an urge comes on you to bathe in the water, but heroic modesty overcomes your desire, as the maidens of Mycenae work beside the bank. Go to **73**.

194

The captain decides to keep close to the shore, and announces his intention of calling at Crommyon to collect more passengers, and bring on board some wine to deliver at Athens. When you reach the port, it is relatively quiet and late afternoon. As you step ashore the captain hails you, saying that the ship will stay in port for two hours, and leave as the sun begins to set. Go to **100**.

195

Is Altheus such a coward that he is afraid even while single-handedly scouting a hostile camp in the dark? Perhaps the shadows frighten you. Whatever the cause, you must take 1 Shame point and lose 1 Honour point. Go to **222**.

196

As you step aside to avoid the horse, you see that on its back there is a majestic rider, wearing flowing robes. As he passes, you hear him laugh and mutter, 'Not half the man his brother was.' With that he rides straight into the sea, and is gone. You carry on past Cenchraea to Crommyon. Go to **100**.

197

The two seem convinced and invite you to sit with them. They order some wine from the innkeeper, and pour some into their goblets.

Do you join in, and drink with them (**140**)?
Or do you refuse their drink (**351**)?

198

The sun lights up the whole city with a harsh glare as it reflects off the newly formed puddles. The water drips rhythmically from the roofs, and slowly the city reawakens, like a thousand squirrels emerging from their winter's rest. The road turns sharply to the right, but there is also a narrower street straight on.

Will you go straight ahead (**109**)?
Or do you follow the road to the right (**440**)?

199

The room is small and dingy. There is no bed. Instead, there is a mattress on the floor, seeming almost alive. Exhausted, you fall asleep despite the squalor, forgetting to pray to your patron. Go to **446**.

200

After some searching, you find an inn which is sumptuous and well furnished. Perhaps this is why there are no other guests. You eat and drink deeply with your host, displaying great *laevendia*, and then stumble to your room and collapse on the bed. Your feet stick out over the end but you manage to curl up and get comfortable. If your patron god is Apollo, turn to **55**. Otherwise, you become sleepy (turn to **500**).

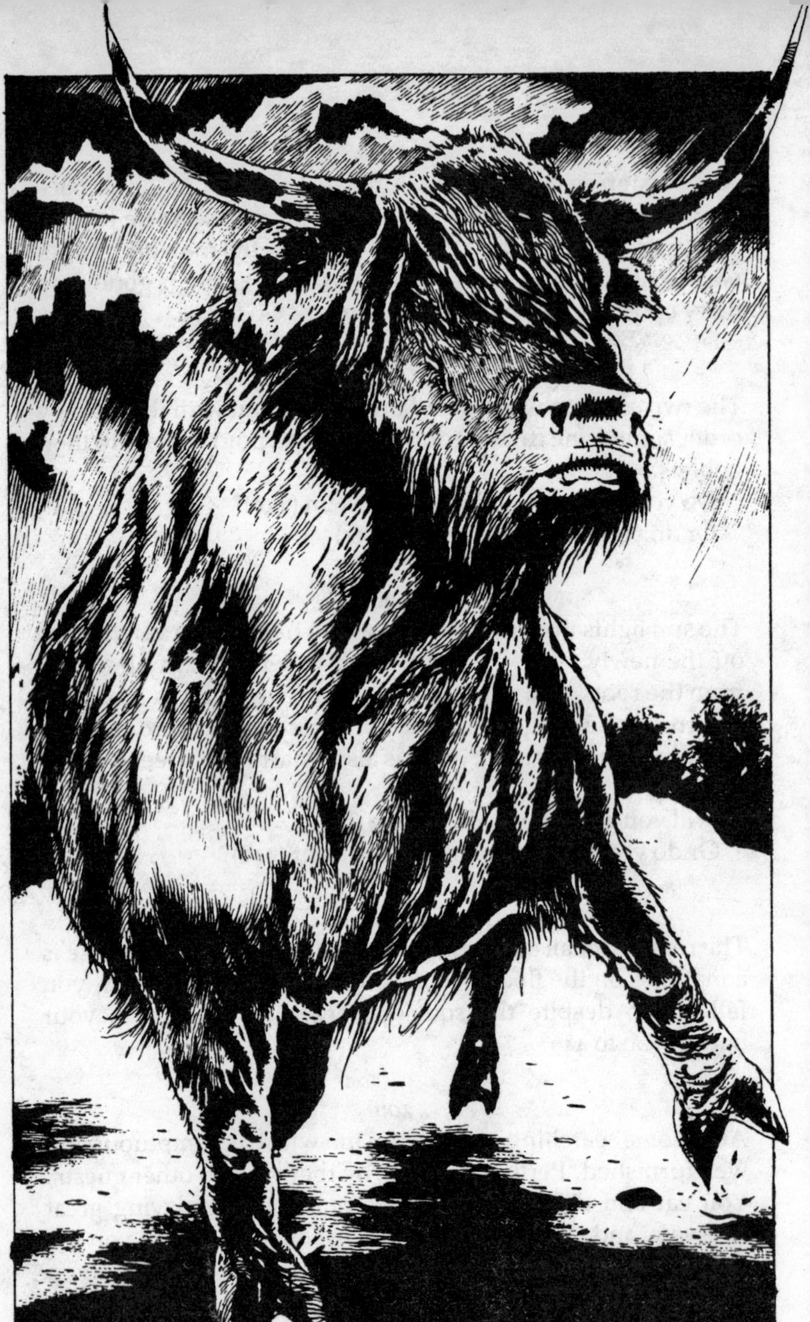

201

You are on the very outskirts of the town, and the people seem to be waving their arms from their huts in warning. You hear a great bellowing noise behind you, and spin around, but too late: the Marathonian bull, the greatest of its kind, is upon you, horns wellnigh as long as a man's arm, its body built as powerfully as the walls of far-off Ilium. Yet you are quick, amicable Altheus, and manage to spring aside, but in doing so you stumble, fall and injure your sword-arm. You are not actually Wounded, but for this combat only, your Might is reduced by 2 points. The bull is Might 10, Protection 16.

If you defeat this infernal creature, turn to **225**.

If you retreat, and refuse to face the task your father has set, turn to **515**.

If you die, but can be saved by Zeus, turn to **47**.

202

Out of the corner of your mouth you pray to your patron god, and hear a soft voice whispering, 'Don't know. It's a mystery to me!' Lose 1 Honour point. Go to **182**.

203

You offer prayers to white-armed Hera, wife of Olympian Zeus, and then set out for Athens, where your father is king. Turn to **2**.

204

The activity in the city begins to die down as dusk approaches, but even now it is bigger than any place you could once have imagined. You wander about, admiring the marvels of the town, not realizing how late it is. With a shock you find it is nearly dark, and you must find an inn before they close their doors for the night. You go down a dark alleyway, thinking you saw an inn-sign at the end of it. Go to **16**.

205

Is amicable Altheus afraid even of the dark, and being alone? Lose 1 Honour point, and return to **185**.

206

The lord of Pagae takes you to a derelict barn on the outskirts of the city. 'Here,' he says, 'the rats are nesting. I am sure that you can deliver us. You have some of the marks of a hero.' With this he ushers you into the barn and closes the door behind you. It is dark and musty, and as your eyes grow accustomed to the gloom, you think you see small shapes scurrying around. There is the sound of squeaking and scrabbling. If you are in Favour with Asclepius, go to **187**. If Asclepius is Neutral to you, or you are in Disfavour, go to **369**.

207

As you come near, you find to your embarrassment that you spent most of your money on the room, and you cannot match the young noblemen's wagers.

Will you offer a gift instead (**113**)?
Or simply watch the races as a spectator (**9**)?

208

The wolf has Might 2, Protection 12. Being an animal, it will not surrender. If you kill it, go to **400**. If you die, but Zeus resurrects you, go to **277**. It is now too late for retreat.

209

The swineherd, on hearing your request, laughs heartily, for he, as he confides, is the royal swineherd. He proffers a scarred and greasy hand, but you do not take it. Sighing, he says that he will take you to the palace, but you must be quick, as he cannot leave the pigs for long. Go to **588**.

210

You stumble backwards, desperately seeking to evade the bear. You catch your ankle in a hole and fall badly. The bear overtakes you, and growling in triumph, lands a mighty blow on your leg. You must take a wound. Return to **616**, and choose again.

211

The city is extremely busy. People flock to and from the vast market. You stand and shake your head at the tradesmen hawking goods from all parts of Greece. City life is so different from the tranquillity of simple Troezen. Standing over the market and dominating it is a temple of Aphrodite, its columns carved in pure white marble, young women and priestesses languishing idly on the steps. You hurry by, and go up to a stall selling fruit. You buy some grapes, and the stall-keeper at once notices that your money is not that of Corinth. You fall into conversation with him. Thinking that you are travelling south, he warns you to avoid Epidaurus, and a man named Procrustes in Tiryns. When you explain your destination, he suggests that you go to Delphi, to seek inspiration from Apollo the prophet god. Another nearby stall-keeper suggests Crommyon as a suitable next stage on your journey. From there, he says, you could catch a boat to Athens.

Do you go through Pagae to Delphi (**302**), to Crommyon (**189**), or stay in Corinth for the night (**204**)?

212

Having completed the corn rite, you must now attend to the water.

Do you drink the water (**607**)?
Do you quench the fire with the water (**356**)?
Or do you sprinkle the water on the seed (**101**)?

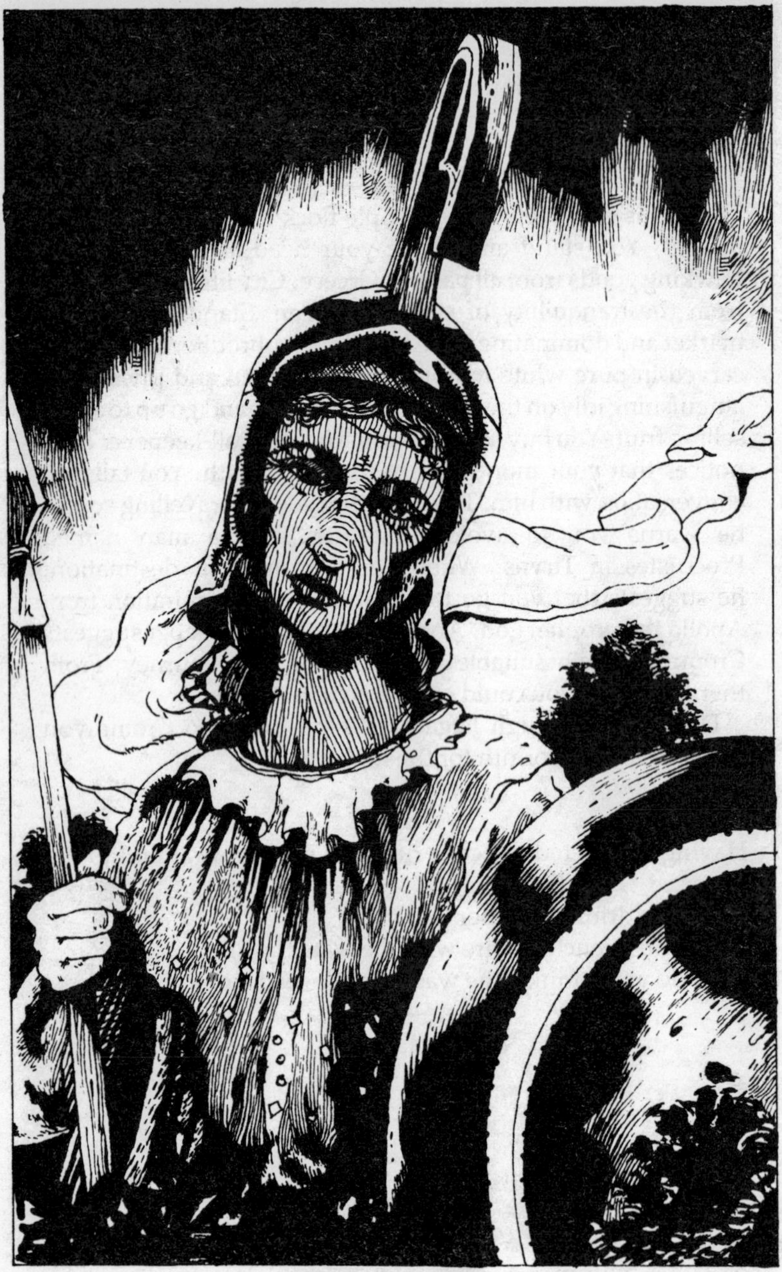

213

'You have done well, Altheus,' says Athena from behind a bush where she has materialized. 'You have fweed Pagae from the tewwible wats. I gweet you, Altheus, as a bwave hewo.' Then she leaves for her shining town of Athens, careful to avoid passing over the barn. You are now in Athena's Favour. Go to 51.

214

An embittered old woman shouts angrily back, 'The Cretans take our young men and maidens to feed to the Minotaur. Do you now ask why we bear a blood-grudge against them? Perhaps you, too, are a Cretan.' With this she picks up a large rock and lobs it at you. It misses, but acts as a signal and soon a shower of stones of varying sizes rains down all about you. Unable to escape, you are hit by one after another.

A great rock smashes your head, and your brain opens and scatters its fluid over the cobbled street. Altheus is no more, unless you can still pray to Zeus. If so, you find yourself at paragraph 394.

215

You silently curse those who threaten their enemies only when weight of numbers is behind them, but prudence prevails, and you hand over the sum they demand. Perhaps one day you will meet one of them alone, and then he will feel the anger of Altheus. You carry on into Cirrha, fury in your heart. Go to 92.

216

A mountain lion roars in the distance, and you hurry onwards, anxious to accomplish the task. The temple is much closer now, and you can see a statue of the god, its face convulsed, as if in mortal pain. The fountain of Asclepius flows red with blood.

Amazed at this sacrilege, your limbs tremble, and you are filled with a divine fury. Onwards you rush into the temple precinct, bellowing strange words as you go, words which come from the gods, like a boar, speared in the frenzied chase, cries out its defiance against the high-hearted hunters: 'Desecrating curs, the god will punish you for your pitiful pride, thinking that you could defile his temple, and escape the price.'

At this, two bandits step forward from the gloom, where once Asclepius' light shone, saying nothing; you know that you must retreat or fight.

If you attempt to retreat now (you may not do so later), go to **145**.

If you attack, go to **388**.

217

Greek wines were never very notable, especially in this period. Lose 1 Honour point, and return to **197**.

218

From the dead queen's arm, you roughly rip a golden amulet, thinking it would be a good present for your mother on your return. As a token of your victory you wear it on your own arm. Turn to **597**.

219

You go up to the stall, and then rather tentatively, when you think no one is looking, you pick up a small loaf and try to conceal it in your tunic. You feel as if everyone in the marketplace turns to look at you, yet no one moves. Perhaps you have escaped. To find out if anyone has noticed, roll one die. On 5 or 6, go to **460**. On 1–4, go to **38**.

220

Before the powers of Sleep brush closed your eyelids, you open a cupboard to put your clothes away, and see there a heap of human skulls. The innkeeper must be a mass murderer! As you hear footsteps approaching, you shut the cupboard and hide behind the door, seizing your club. Turn to **272**.

221

You lose 1 Honour point for attacking an opponent from behind, but in the time you gain you manage to inflict a Wound on one of the brigands. Go to **462**.

222

Closer you creep, like the mountain lion that stalks her prey, craving meat for her hungry cubs crying out in the den. There are few guards: the Amazons seem too confident for such a precaution. You look into one tent. Fortunately, it is not occupied, and there is little of interest, only various jars, urns and a shield of sewn hides. Before you can examine this more closely, you hear voices: someone is about to enter the tent.

'Queen Antiope's leopardskin . . .' the speaker begins, but then sees you and stops. She carries a spear and a sewn-hide shield, and wears a bearskin.

Do you attack this tall, powerful Amazon before she can call for aid (**544**)?

Or do you try to escape out of the other end of the tent (**343**)?

223

In the morning the goddess is gone. You leave the house and carry on out of the city. Go to **263**.

224

No hero would allow himself to be set upon by peasants in a dark alleyway. You notice some men lurking there, and quickly move on, wondering at men who will attack from behind, like dogs or Trojans, typical of city-dwellers. Go to **331**.

225

The bull makes one last feeble attempt to impale you on its horns, but then collapses, heaves one last rasping breath, and is dead. You cut off a piece of its horns as token of your victory, and, elated, turn away and set off down the road back to Athens, not waiting even to receive the gratitude of the people of Marathon.

You may have 7 Honour points. Go to **456**.

226

Even to think of shedding blood in the house of your father is shameful, especially since you have lied about your name and parentage. Take 2 Shame points. You realize that resisting will simply bring more guards, so you surrender. You are handled roughly and bundled into a cell near the entrance, and you languish there in the dark, confused at the reception you have been given. Go to **185**.

227

The dark wine spills on the table and runs down, soiling the tunic of a Phoenician trader who is seated next to you. You apologize profusely for your clumsiness. Take 1 Shame point. King Aegeus notices you, and gestures to you. Turn to **170**.

228

You are now in Disfavour with Asclepius (record this on your Chronicle Sheet). You carry on a little way from the town, and there rest for the night, before continuing on to Cleonae. Turn to **536**.

229

Lose 1 Honour point, and take 1 Shame point. Go to **588**.

230

At length you reach the slope of the hill on which the citadel stands. It is steep, and you are forced to stop several times. The houses here are much older than those below, and their denizens richer, but nowhere here can your father's palace be discerned. You reach the summit, and pass through the gates where the guards stand with great body-shields and ceremonial armour. They do not stop you. You clamber up the wall on the other side of the gate to get a better look at the city below. Go to **49**.

231

You take a swipe at one of the creatures, but miss, and they retire to a nearby tree. Then, as one, they come screaming to the attack. The man, meanwhile, cowers in the gloom, too frightened to move.

There are three Furies: Tisiphone, Alecto and Megaera. They fight in that order. Each has Might 4, Protection 18 (but remember the bonus to Might for multiple opponents).

If you surrender, go to **153**.
If you retreat, go to **520**.
If you die, and pray to be saved by Zeus, go to **463**.
If you Seriously Wound a Fury, go to **83**.

232

You awaken next morning, your head throbbing. The events of last night seem long ago, and such indulgence is not fitting for a hero with great deeds to accomplish. Have 2 Shame points, but you are in Favour with Dionysus, god of the vine. At length, after an hour's walk, you find the road to Thebes. Go to **13**.

233

The beggar thanks you heartily, and the gods smile on your pity for a fellow mortal, pushed down by the cares of the world. For your act they award you 1 Honour point. Out of Mycenae you walk, keenly aware of the cruelty of city-dwelling men. Go to **536**.

234

At length, you are ordered to serve at the table. Into your hands is placed the huge brazen mixing-bowl you had cleaned, now filled with wine. Into the hall you are hustled, and there

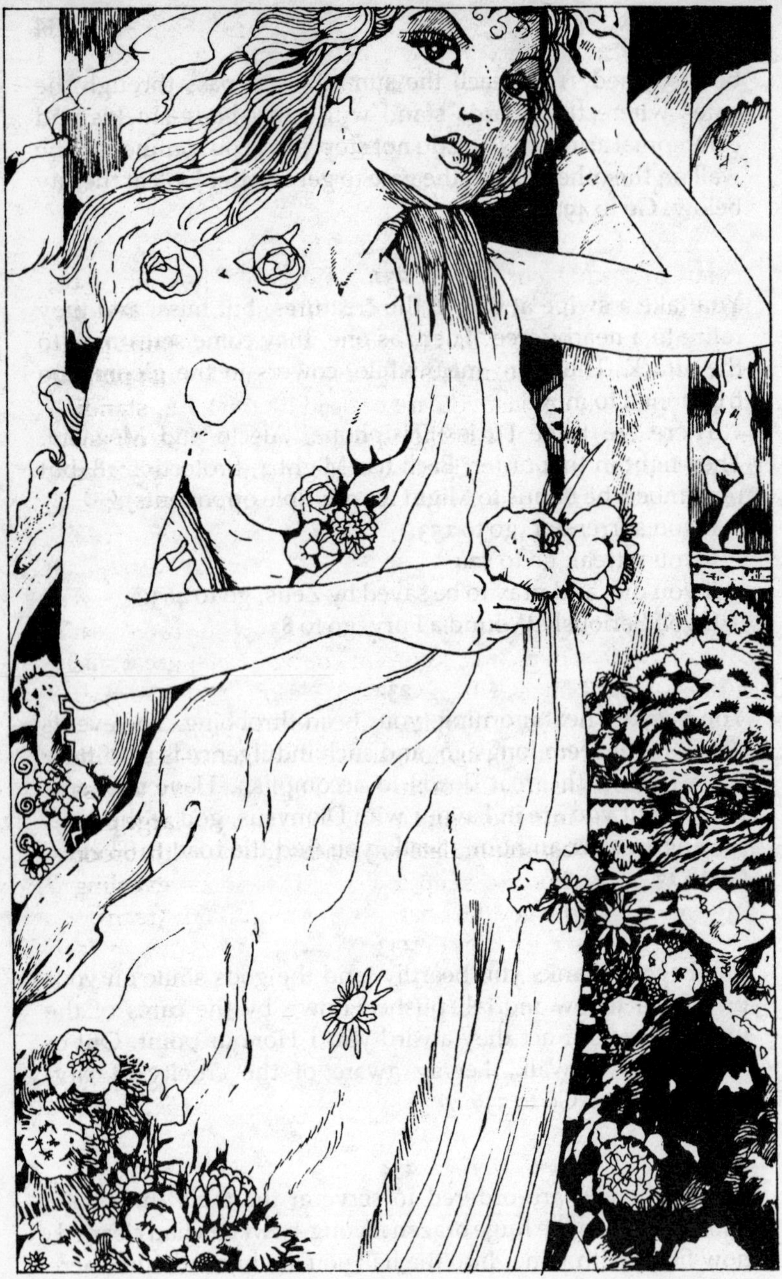

set out before you is a splendid scene. All the guests of the
king, the nobility of Athens, and even the king's retainers and
servants are seated around a huge table. You set down the
bowl and from it wine is drawn for the goblets. Once a portion
of the food has been set aside for Athena, protectress of the
city, to be burnt later, the feast begins. You see more meat,
bread and wine consumed than you could possibly have
imagined existed. There are men from Laconia, Boeotia,
Thessaly, even some from Phoenicia, whence the ships ply to
and fro across the ocean. It is the custom that all must partake
of the feast, and at last you are noticed by the king, standing
away in the corner. He beckons you to him, breaks off some
bread from his plate and gives it to you. You must take 3 Shame
points for the humiliation of acting as a servant in your father's
house. Turn to **383**.

235

The palace is voluptuously furnished, with huge satin
cushions, vases depicting scenes of young lovers, great silken
curtains, and statues of the goddess in various poses. At the far
wall, beneath one vast marble sculpture of herself, Aphrodite
sits on a pink coloured cushion, surrounded by flowers. Every
so often she picks up one of these and sniffs it, only to toss it
carelessly away into the centre of the floor, where a large pile of
these blooms has accumulated. Handmaidens with brooms
sweep the vast floor to keep it clear, sometimes revealing a
huge mosaic of the goddess bathing in a mountain stream.

'Altheus,' she coos, yet her voice carries across the palace
room, 'I do hope you've been keeping well. *I* have. Anyway,
before we get down to talking about interesting things, like
me, I ought to tell you about this huge bronze giant named
Talos who walks around Crete four times a day. Just before
noon, strike east, and you'll catch him out around the other
side. Be a good boy and don't forget about Ariadne.' With this
she tosses one last red poppy to the floor.

You feel yourself carried back to the shore, where you stand,
astonished and tired. The sailors greet you with amazement,

for you have been gone several days. On hearing your tale, they are still more perplexed at having an honoured one of the goddess among them. Go to **583**.

236

Through the winding streets you rush, and at last come to the palace. A spacious colonnade adorns the front with columns of marble. Baskets of flowers around the door fill the air with a sweet-smelling fragrance. At the gate stands a guard, forbidding entrance to all unauthorized people. He looks hot, clad in armour and carrying a short spear. You approach him and demand entrance, but he simply looks at you sidelong.

'What is your name?' he sneers.

Do you reply 'Styrikon' (**164**), 'Altheus' (**328**), or 'Pyraphas' (**87**)?

237

You rest, and in the morning continue on your way, completely refreshed. Turn to **2**.

238

It does not take you long to find a hostelry no more appealing than the rest of the town, but you wait for some time before the surly innkeeper will serve you. The food gets worse with every mouthful, and at the end the keeper belches in your face.

You pay him more than the whole tavern is worth, and resolve to wait out the night here. You doze lightly, and, as if in a dream, hear fragments of conversation from the other customers.

'. . . I was going to the bear-hunt, but apparently some fool killed it last night . . .'

'. . . I used to be one of hers, but the lisp put me right off . . .'

'. . . I've told the other five. The assassin strikes at . . .'

Go to **70**.

239

You have only yourself to blame for this situation. Lose 1 Honour point and go back to **219**. If you choose instead to spend the rest of your life stealing from the markets of Megara, go to **5**.

240
You approach the conspirators and explain that you have heard everything. You say that you have a grudge against the king of Thebes, and would like to help if you can. The men look startled, and whisper to each other.

If your patron is Ares, Hera or Poseidon, go to **354**.
If your patron is Apollo, Aphrodite, or Athena, go to **197**.
If you have no patron, go to **354**.

241
The guard motions to a passing kitchen-boy, who runs off breathless. Not long afterwards he returns, and speaks frantically with the guard. You listen, and with joy in your heart realize that you are to be released, for the king is holding a great feast today, and it would be shameful to keep a man prisoner, and not to share the meal with him. Turn to **350**.

242

Pious words wing from your mouth to high Olympus. 'If ever you have heard me before, now is the time to aid me,' you pray, but there is no response. Have 1 Honour point. When you look up, the Amazon has gone, taking advantage of your prayer to escape.

Do you stride boldly out of the front of the tent, seeking to continue the battle (**613**)?

Or do you escape out of the back of the tent (**259**)?

243

The inn is crowded, but the daughter of the owner brings you an urn filled with wine, and pours some into your gold-rimmed goblet. Like the hum of bees, the conversation drones on, but you are too tired to listen. At length soft Sleep conquers the resolve of your strong-built limbs. When you wake, the captain and all the other customers have gone. You rouse yourself, and make unsteadily for the door, your mind clouded, as if the wine was drawn from the waters of Lethe. At the door there are two tables, one on either side, on which lie piles of documents, undoubtedly private. You could read them, but if you were caught, yours would be the punishment of the thief, or the coward who lurks in the dark.

Do you look at the documents on the right-hand table (go to **173**)?

Do you decide not to sully your honour, and return to the ship (go to **326**)?

Or do you choose to examine the left-hand documents (go to **368**)?

244

Ahead of you, you can now see a large group of people, some ten or fifteen strong. They shout and wail, while the women in the party tear their hair and their black shawls. They appear to be carrying some large object, but you cannot make out what it is, since the dust and haze obscure your view.

Do you move closer, and investigate the reason for this disturbance (go to **494**)?

Or do you turn aside a while from the path to the Acropolis, and avoid the crowd altogether (**78**)?

245

Fear in the face of victory? Lose 1 Honour point, and go to **456**.

246

Ah, amicable Altheus, who would have thought it? Offering an item you do not possess. Have 1 Shame point, and choose again at **113**.

247

You wake from an unconscious trance, cold and half dead. You have been washed up on the shore, you know not how. After the storm and the swim towards shore, you find yourself weaponless. 'Where is this place?' you think to yourself. You must find some settlement soon or you will die. The sun dries your skin, and your flesh begins to burn under its hot rays. At the summit of a nearby hill, you hear the sound of tinkling bells, and think you see a farmer with his herd of goats. You rush as fast as you can to the place, but when you get there the man has gone. Below you can see a small town, its green fields laid out, and the peasants working there, as ants store up food for the winter. You continue down on the road. Go to **100**.

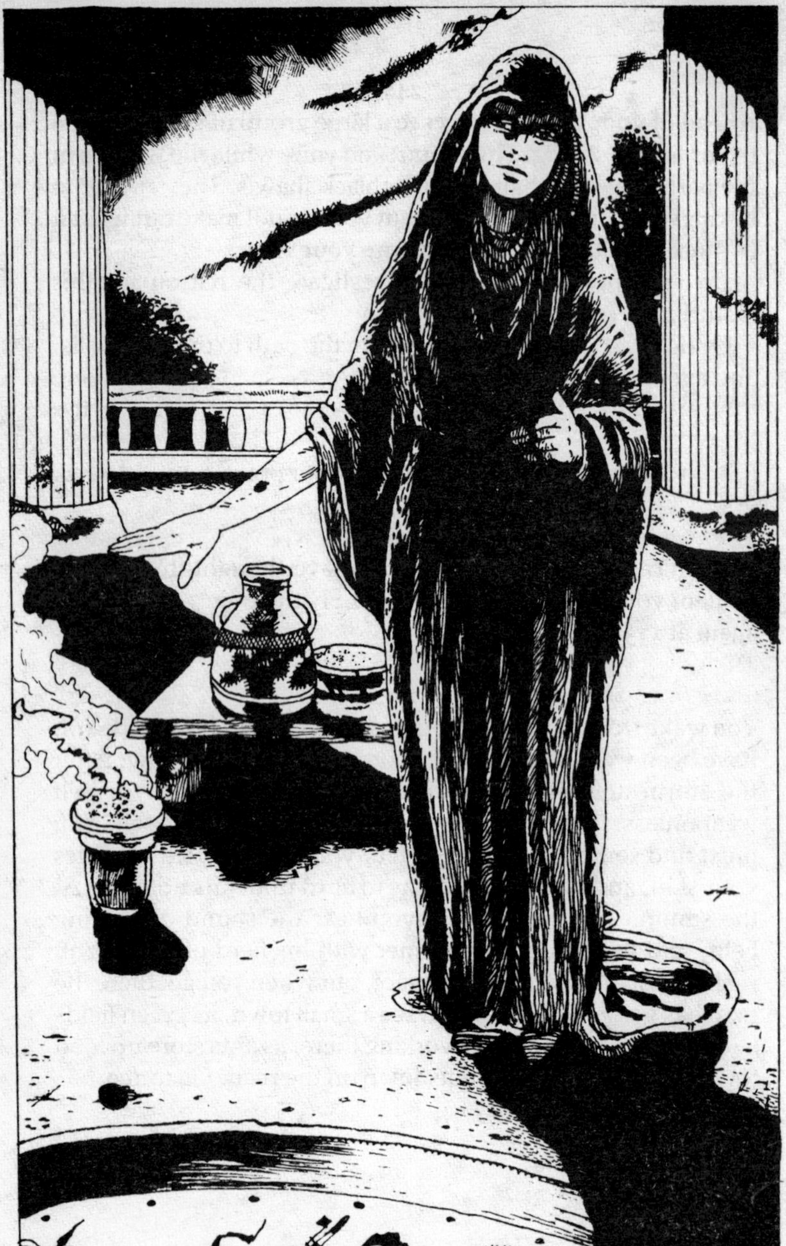

248

Before you are fully aware of what is going on, you are on top of the temple. The priestess speaks to the people, 'Citizens of Eleusis, worshippers of Demeter, as is the goddess's will, it is one of the common people who officiates at the springtime rite of corn, water and flame, the symbols of rebirth. Let the rites begin.' The priestess steps aside to reveal a low table on which stand an urn of water, a bowl of corn seed, and a small brazier on which a blue-white flame is burning.

There is no backing out now; you must somehow complete the ceremony. Do you deal with the corn first (**182**), or the water (**58**)?

249

You rush out into the corridor, and there you see five guards, none of them heavily armed, for they have run straight from the barracks. Each has a shortsword (Might 2, Protection 0), and a breastplate (Might 0, Protection 3). Their basic values are Might 3, Protection 11, making Might 5, Protection 14 in all (but Might 9 for the first, 8 for the second, etc.)

They rush in screaming, 'No quarter, regicide!' Clearly no surrender is possible.

If you are victorious, go to **267**.

If you retreat, go to **472**.

If you die and are saved by Zeus, you find yourself at **134**.

250

You must expend 1 to 6 Honour points (roll a die). If you cannot afford this, lose 1 Honour point and return to **422**. If you can, then your patron has thrown up the blood of the fountain into the men's faces, and you have enough time to rush back down the path away from Epidaurus, but not enough to collect your weapons and armour before they recover. Go to **536**.

251

As rosy-fingered Dawn, daughter of Morning, finally touches the sky, and performs her appointed office, you come across a glade, strewn with broken goblets and empty wineskins. You carry on, and a little way along you find a dead bear.

If Artemis is your patron, go to **311**.

Otherwise, go to **265**.

252
Have 2 Shame points for killing an opponent who has surrendered. Leaving the clearing, you come upon a large group of Amazons. Seeking to avert the plottings of Eris, the bringer of strife, you start to explain your mission, but they see that you have slaughtered their sister. Maddened with rage, they charge, and it is with difficulty that you elude them, and make your way at a run towards Athens. Turn to **165**.

253
'Then take a gift from me, amicable Altheus – my curse.' Before you can wonder how the old man knew your name, he has fled into the bushes, and away to the central part of the island. Lose 1 Honour point, and go to **583**.

254
The temple is a small and simple affair. 'The priest is not here. He died at the hands of the Hellish Man,' explains an elder. 'There will be no more prophecies on Delos, until the god touches one of us with that gift and curse which bestows great honour and takes away all peace.'

If Apollo is your patron, or you are in Favour with him, go to **305**.

If Apollo is Neutral to you, go to **552**.

If you are in Disfavour with him, go to **360**.

255
For a man of your heroic stature, refusal to accept the hospitality of a host and the dishonour of sleeping like a beggar or a slave among the dogs are unworthy indeed. You therefore must lose 2 Honour points. In the morning you go on towards Cleonae. Go to **536**.

256

Can you not speak? Do you require the help of the gods to remember your name? Have 1 Shame point, and return to **236**.

257

The ship is tossed about like a bunch of grapes thrown from hand to hand amongst the joyous pickers. To the very crown of heaven it is cast, and then down into the churning waters. A huge wave rears up and sends its white spray-foaming water crashing down on the hollow vessel. The boat's sturdy sides splinter in shards of flying wood, mingled with the sea-snapped bones of the crew. You too, amicable Altheus, do not escape the carnage, for you are its cause. Shame and the death-bringing waters of the wave lord overwhelm you.

258

You are awake now, and strain to hear. As you listen, it becomes clear that a plot is afoot to kill the king of Thebes. You can let sleeping dogs lie (go to **70**), or take the part of the king (go to **64**) or of the conspirators (go to **240**).

259

When you emerge, you find that you are surrounded by a group of some twenty of the warrior women. You cannot resist and they catch you, strip you of all your weapons and armour, and send you off with only a loincloth to protect you from the night air's bitter cold. 'That,' jeers one, 'is your reward for invading our camp like a wolf or thief.' Lose 4 Honour points, and go to **320**.

260

The pilgrims, seeing that you are a man of violence, readily give up a small effigy of the god Apollo, begging you to spare their lives. Aware already of the offence against Apollo that you have committed in seeking to assault pilgrims on the way to his shrine, you desist, and move quickly past the frightened band of men and women. As you start again down the road, you can hear them in the distance, cursing you, and calling on Apollo to punish you. You are now in Disfavour with Apollo. If he is your patron, lose 2 Honour points instead. It is late as you approach the town of Cirrha. Turn to **339**.

261

As you approach the far bank, you hear the woman shouting, but as you listen, the rasping voice is transformed into sweet, lyrical speech. You look back. This is no woman, it is the goddess Hera: 'Ignore me now, but some day you will have to pay me homage.' You are now in Disfavour with Hera. Go to **294**.

262

The bearskin-clad warrior is Might 7, Protection 14.

If you die, and are saved by Zeus, turn to **180**.
If you retreat, turn to **275**.
If you surrender, turn to **355**.
If you Seriously Wound her, turn to **375**.

263

You leave high-walled Tiryns far behind you as, mulling over the night's events in your mind, you journey north to Mycenae. The road is high-banked, and there are few travellers. Some hours pass, and you reach a place where a track joins the road. Unsure of your route, you question a passing farmer, on his way to the market at Tiryns. He tells you that the track leads east to Epidaurus, home of Asclepius the healer, but that the road leads as you thought to Mycenae the lion city.

If you take the track to Epidaurus, go to **324**; otherwise you carry on to Mycenae (**503**).

264

The gods are pleased at your bravery, but even a hero cannot defeat twenty well-armed men. Have 1 Honour point, and either pay the money (go to **215**), or agree to yoke the bull (go to **413**).

265
Leaving the bear behind, you proceed. The road curves gently to the right. A strap on your sandal snaps, and you are forced to spend some time repairing it. The trees seem much less threatening, and at length the road joins another. Go to **13**.

266
The innkeeper welcomes you in when you knock, smiles and beckons you towards a room. You choose to have a meal first, and retire, contented, to a good night's rest. In the morning you eat a hearty breakfast, and carry on out of the town. Go to **3**.

267
You may have 8 Honour points for defeating the guards. You make your escape out of the window, as you can hear more guards making their way up the stairs to the corridor. Go to **472**.

268
You have almost reached Crommyon, and the farmer informs you that you must get off now, as he must visit a friend. He gives you a large hunk of cheese; you thank him, and he drives off along a track. You walk along past the first houses, which have smoke drifting from their chimneys, spiralling lazily, as a bird in flight. You enter Crommyon itself. Go to **100**.

269
You take a handful of corn seed from the bowl, lift it to your mouth and begin to eat. The crowd gasps in horror at what you have done. Go to **120**.

270
You enter the kitchen. In front of you a vast feast is being prepared. Huge cauldrons of bronze bubble with stews, and a great boar's head on a platter is ready to be served. There is bread and wine in great quantity. In one corner a woman

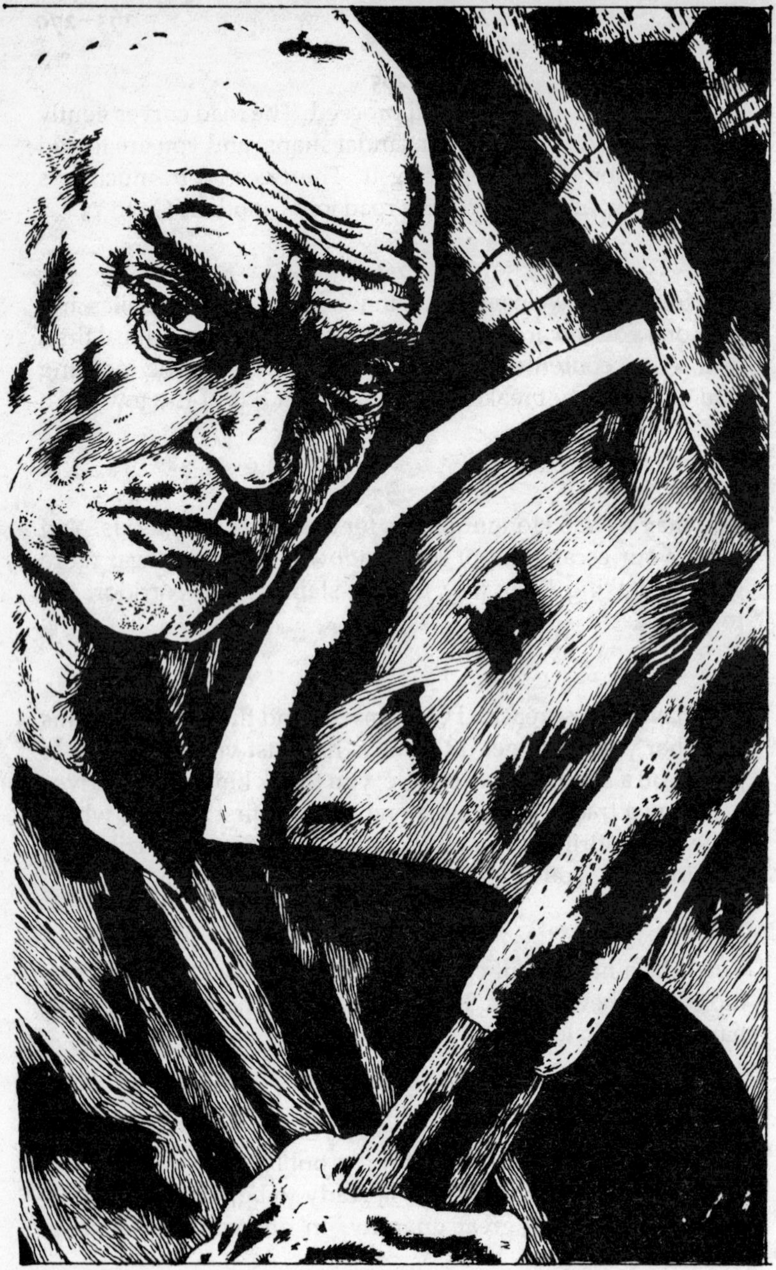

weaves on a loom; in another a young boy scrubs at a table ornament of beaten gold. This kitchen seems far grander than the whole of your mother Aethra's house in far-off Troezen. Go to **382**.

271

Your horse reaches the finish-line panting. No one is at hand to congratulate you. They are all cheering the victor. He has a wreath of laurel leaves adorning his brow. Dejected, you slip away back to the inn, dreaming of wheels and hoofs, forgetful of your ordained quest and wishing that the winner's crown might have been yours.

You lose 2 Honour points, and in the morning you awaken, stiff and sore, and set out to Athens. Turn to **474**.

272

The innkeeper enters with an axe in his hand. When he sees nobody in the bed, he gasps and looks wildly around. Shouting the battle-cry of your people, you attack him, take him by surprise and inflict one Wound. Then the battle starts, with you striking first. Procrustes is Might 1, Protection 10, and his axe is Might 5, Protection −3. Cornered in the room, you cannot retreat.

If he is Seriously Wounded, go to **21**.

If you surrender, go to **571**.

If you die, and Zeus saves you, go to **263**.

273

The Amazon drops her strong-shafted spear to the ground, unable to fight any longer. 'Be merciful,' she cries, 'and Hera will smile on you.'

Do you spare her (**507**), or kill her anyway (**516**)?

274

You feebly stammer out that you have spared the men, and they have escaped. 'You waste my time,' replies the king. 'Lock him in the storeroom. In the morning we will have a public flogging. I think I shall officiate.' Go to **433**.

275

Take 1 extra Shame point for retreating and abandoning the fight for your father's city. A short while after you leave the battle, it is clear that the Athenians are losing, so you enter the fray once more. Return to **102**, and choose a different opponent.

276

Stung by what seems like a multitude of bees, you decide that the honey is not worth the price that all-seeing Zeus has decreed you must pay. You can either go back to the ship and await the casting off from Melos (**595**), or you could attempt with some of the other sailors to kill one of the cows, so that you may have fresh meat (**59**).

277

You come at last to the town of Epidaurus. You look around in amazement at the crowded streets. Unfamiliar faces push past you and crush you against the high-towered walls. No one stops or notices you, and they all seem miserable, as if abandoned by the gods. Eventually courage builds itself in your mind, and you seek to converse with a high-born lady. She ignores you with a contemptuous glance. Almost in despair you seize a passer-by, and shake his arm. 'Friend,' you say, 'where is the inn? Why is the town so afflicted? Is Olympian Zeus angry with its people? Do the Harpies visit your feast-tables, laden with the fruits of the earth?'

The man only shakes his head and points lamely ahead. You look and see a scruffy tavern. You turn to question the man, but he has scurried off. Resigned, you walk towards the small, squat building. The steps are unwashed, and the windows are caked with dirt. A sign above the door tells you that it is indeed a place where you can find a room for the night.

Do you go in (go to **36**)?
Or do you go away (go to **341**)?

278

Aphrodite is your mistress, and you have failed to honour beauty; you have failed to see the truth. Until you reach Crete Aphrodite is no longer considered to be your patron. Have 6 Shame points, and go to **608**.

279

You reach the harbour. As you approach the place where Athena's proud vessel lies, you feel inside your tunic and find that the documents for great Minos, king of Crete, have gone. You have failed your father if you do not find them. The ship must sail soon, and you have little time.

Do you investigate the inn of Cythnos (**380**), or a large white-washed house near by (**545**)?

280

The portly cook looks slyly at you and says, 'So you're Altheus, son of Aegeus.' Seeing you nod, she scurries away and screams 'Guards, arrest this man!' Before you have time to escape, or even get into the kitchen and through to the palace, two sword-armed guards with body-length shields have set upon you.

They are Might 5, Protection 14 (basic Might 3, Protection 10, plus sword of Might 3, plus great shield of Might −1, Protection 4). Remember the rules for fighting multiple opponents.

If you die and are saved by Zeus, turn to **166**.
If you surrender, turn to **457**.
If you retreat, turn to **289**.
When both men are Seriously Wounded, turn to **119**.

281

You make your way to the palace and, as you had been told, a side entrance has been left open. You sneak through the courtyard to the door, and climb the staircase beyond it. You come to a high-ceilinged corridor; frescoes adorn its walls, but you pay them no heed, intent as you are on your task. Soon you come to the door of the king's bed-chamber; it is unguarded. You lift the latch and enter.

The king is asleep, and snoring loudly. Beside him lies a great longsword in its scabbard. He fingers it in his sleep and seems to stir. You rush up to the bed and raise the dagger the conspirators gave to you. Go to **24**.

282

With one last thrust you bring low the great creature, unstringing the force that binds its mighty sinews, and with one last roar it collapses dead. You are the victor, but you do not wait for the crown, impatient in your heart to be in Athens once more. You wait only long enough to sever a portion of the horn as proof of your valour, and are off, back to high-towered Athens, and the palace of your father. You may have 7 Honour points. Go to **456**.

283

Back from the battlefield you come, bloodied but not beaten. Yours is the victory. You come to the great feasting-hall of Aegeus, where most of the warriors are gathered, mourning the dead, but rejoicing in their hearts that the warlike Amazons have been thrown back to their ships. In the background, servants scurry to and fro, preparing a victory feast. The gathered company cheers you for your part in the fight, as men at oars cheer the helmsman who has guided them safe through the jagged rocks. Go to **441**.

284

You pull the old man away from the curtain. No one notices, but you feel the favour of the god come upon you. Go to **299**.

285

The door opens, but instead of the greybeard's visage you see a pile of slops hurled towards you from a bucket. You must take 1 Shame point for this humiliation. You become enraged and try to force your way into the inn.

Will you control your anger and go on your way, smelling of the inn's sewage (go to **304**)?

Or do you force your way in to deal with the innkeeper and his friends (go to **192**)?

286

You seem to see the reveller god before you, running in the woods with his maenads in train, like a hunter with his pack of hounds. 'Beware,' he cries, 'or your fate will be that of our prey. The wine is poisoned; do not drink it.' You leave your goblet untouched until the end of the feasting, when the king turns towards you to speak. Turn to **170**.

287

The trader shouts out, 'Stop, thieves!' A general hue and cry erupts as everywhere people rush about seeking to catch the men. You find it surprising that anyone could hope to achieve anything in this mêlée, more reminiscent of the fights of the Achaians under high-walled Troy, but at length the thieves are caught, and taken away by the market-wardens for summary justice. Go to **414**.

288

The injured man snatches the gem eagerly, delighted that you should offer such a treasure. 'Your chariot is red,' he says. Go to **391**.

289

You turn and rush away from your attackers, knocking down a great cauldron of steaming-hot stew. Your leg is scalded, and you fall down at the feet of two more guards who have come upon you from behind, like bandits, or the men of far-off Egypt. You are dragged off, struggling and shouting, amazed at the treatment meted out to you in your father's house. Turn to **459**.

290

Ares the stormer of strong walls appears. 'Pine doors. Not bad. Eliminated the foe. Top marks. Nice finish. Keep it up. Good man.' The god vanishes in a swirl of red smoke. If Ares is not your patron, you are in his Favour and get 3 Honour points. If he is, then you get 5 Honour points. In both cases you have 2 Shame points for killing a man who has surrendered. You spend the night sleeping in the best room of the inn, and none of the guests dares approach you. In the morning you carry on your journey. Go to **3**.

291

The Amazon does not surrender. Remember that she is Might 7, Protection 13.

If you finally kill her, turn to **527**.
If you retreat, turn to **275**.
If you surrender, turn to **355**.
If you die, and are saved by Zeus, turn to **180**.

292

You hand over your weapon uncertainly, and the wise man tosses it to the ground. 'What need of weapons have I,' he shrieks, 'who know the future's vast panorama? Beneath the waves your truest weapon's use does lie.' With this, he laughs maniacally, rolls over twice in a muddy pond, and crawls away into the bush, with speed belying his state. You sigh, pick up your weapon and walk back towards the ship. Have 1 Honour point, and go to **583**.

293

You threaten to kill her if she does not tell you the reason for the attack. She tugs at her long black hair for a moment, as if in thought, and then says, 'It is no secret. Aegeus' soldiers raided our land, and amongst the booty was a golden hairpin sacred to Hera; a small thing to you, but the symbol of our queen's power.' On a whim, you pick up a small silver ear-ring, which has fallen to the floor. Turn to **507**.

294

You struggle across the rest of the river, your tired legs shaking with the cold. You hear something drop in the churning water; perhaps you have dislodged a pebble. At length you struggle up the other bank. Go to **417**.

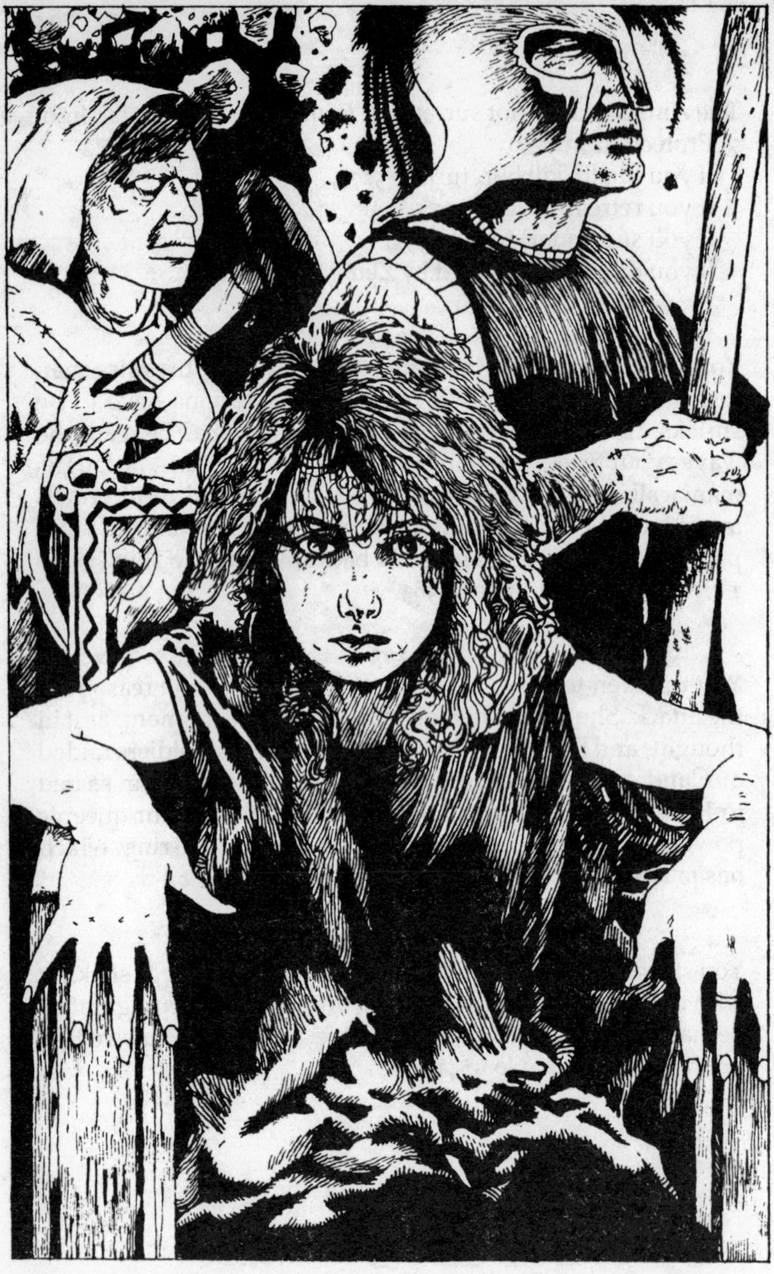

295

You disembark on Thera, which, despite its appearance from afar, seems a gloomy place. You have not been travelling for long when you see a strange sight: a woman on a golden throne is sitting beneath the cliff. Beside her is a proud warrior, bearing a mighty-shafted spear, and standing alongside him is a lame man, dressed in the apron of a blacksmith, bearing a hammer of black metal.

As fast as the thunderflash that comes from Zeus, the cliff begins to crumble. 'Save us,' the figures cry in unison. You are the closest, and have time to save only one.

If Hera is your patron, go to **26**.
If Ares is your patron, go to **139**.
Otherwise, go to **543**.

296

Have 5 Shame points for the refusal even to consider aiding the temple of so great a god. You wait unhappily, aware of your crime, as the ship is provisioned, while the elders look on, astounded at the answer of amicable Altheus. Go to **492**.

297

The temple walls are bare; there are none of the tapestries that decorate the temple at Troezen. The only ornaments are the thousands of gifts heaped in front of the sanctuary of the Pythian priestess. A dull white curtain edged in gold conceals the Pythia from prying eyes.

You see a white-robed priest approach you. He stops in front of you and waits expectantly, and then impatiently. Go to **126**.

298

You rush below decks, frantically trying to reach your weapons before the beast strikes again. You are too late: there is a great crunch, as of the mighty oak which falls, roots torn by great father Zeus' thunderstroke. Water rushes in, and you are carried off into the churning depths.

Roll two dice. If their sum is greater than or equal to the difference between your Honour and Shame, go to **453**. If it is less, go to **477**.

299

The priestess, no longer gripped by the power of the god, falls silent. The priest approaches you once more and says, 'I must interpret for you the words of the prophet god. Thus speaks Apollo:

> *"Go to the daughter of a far-off king,*
> *And put your trust in the sheep's offspring."*'

He grins knowingly, and, having thanked him for the help he has given, you turn, collect your armour and set out down the road to Thebes (**191**).

300

The priestess leaps to your side and exclaims, 'Spring is here! Demeter's daughter Persephone has returned! Rejoice! For the great mother smiles on the earth once more.' With this the festivities begin. Feasting, dancing, singing and celebrations of the fertility goddess are soon under way. It is late in the night when, filled with food and wine, you retire, but are kept awake by the sound of the feasting and the clash of the sacred cymbals.

In the morning you awaken. The celebrations are still continuing, but, before you leave, the high priestess presses a gift into your hands. It is a golden brooch, crafted in the form of an ear of corn. She explains that it will identify you as a friend of the priestesses of Demeter. She then returns once more to the sacred enclosure.

You may have 3 Honour points, and are now in Favour with Demeter. Go to **138**.

301

Seeing that the fight is hopeless, and that you are too lucky, both men drop to their knees and beg for clemency. One of them gasps out, 'Spare us, and we will tell you everything. Kill us, and the blood of the king of Thebes is on your hands, and the implacable Furies will pursue you to the end of your days.' You may have 6 Honour points for your victory, and may take one dagger (Might 1, Protection 0), but may not use it with any other weapon.

Do you spare the men (**429**)?
Or do you kill them anyway (**177**)?

302

The road to Pagae is strewn with the bodies of dead cattle and goats, wasted from the plague, and rotting from days in the sun. The smell is at times overpowering. Unperturbed, you press on, not to be turned aside by some farmer's ill luck. You pass a shrine to Athena, the owl goddess, protectress of this town. The streets seem strangely deserted. As you pass a particularly imposing building, a man beckons to you.

'Stranger,' he calls, 'for you are obviously such, and have not heard of this town's affliction. There is plague here, caused by rats. All our efforts to drive them out have been unsuccessful. Many of our folk have been bitten, and died. Perhaps you could help us.'

Do you leave Pagae as quickly as possible (go to **490**)?
Or do you agree to help Athena's town (go to **206**)?

303

In your hands you hold the cake. On it you smear honey, and over this you pour some milk from a skin at your belt. 'Infernal goddesses, desist, and take instead my offering.' The Furies look annoyed, but fly to the place where you stand, take the cakes with greedy hands, and flap away into the night, screeching: 'You have stopped us once, but this wretch shall not escape.' Lose 1 Honour point for interrupting the course of divine justice. Go to **501**.

304

Red-eyed Ares the battler stands in your way and says, 'Vile coward. No mettle. Pull yourself together. Now on, no disgrace. That is all. Dismissed.' If Ares is not your patron you are in Disfavour with him. If he is, you fight your next battle without the help of his supernatural strength. In both cases, take 1 point of Shame. Go to **23**.

305

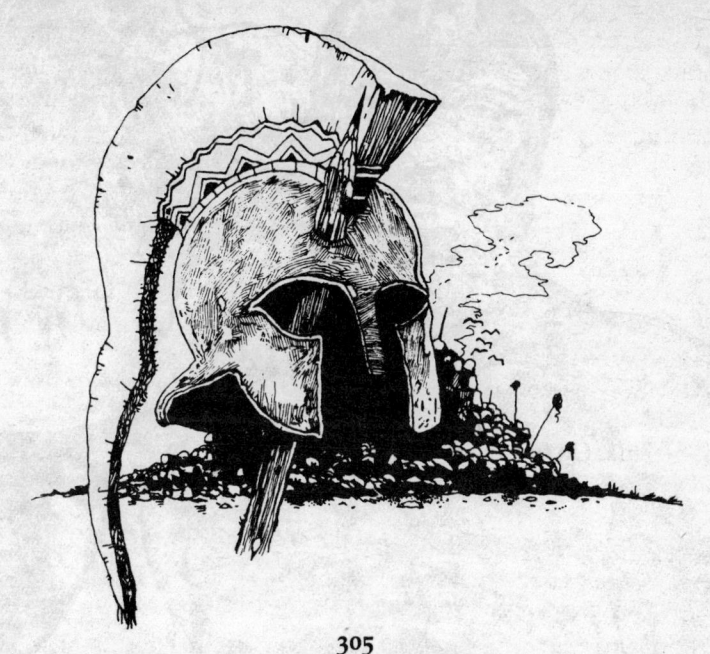

As you turn to leave, there stands before you divine Apollo, robe besmirched and hair unkempt. 'I'm awfully sorry,' he says. 'I got up rather late and almost failed to come. Immortality makes one so sleepy. Oh yes, a prophecy:

> *"Man of bronze beneath the waves,*
> *Sending folk to early graves,*
> *There lies your death."*

Sorry, must dash.' With this, divine Apollo is gone.

Perturbed by the god's actions, you carry on out of the door, and realize that the elders are far in front of you. They cannot have heard Apollo's prophecy. You have to hurry to catch up. Go to **449**.

306

The flame wavers and is extinguished. There is a hissing, and a thick grey smoke rises to the heavens. The crowd cheers, and awaits the next part of the ceremony. Go to **89**.

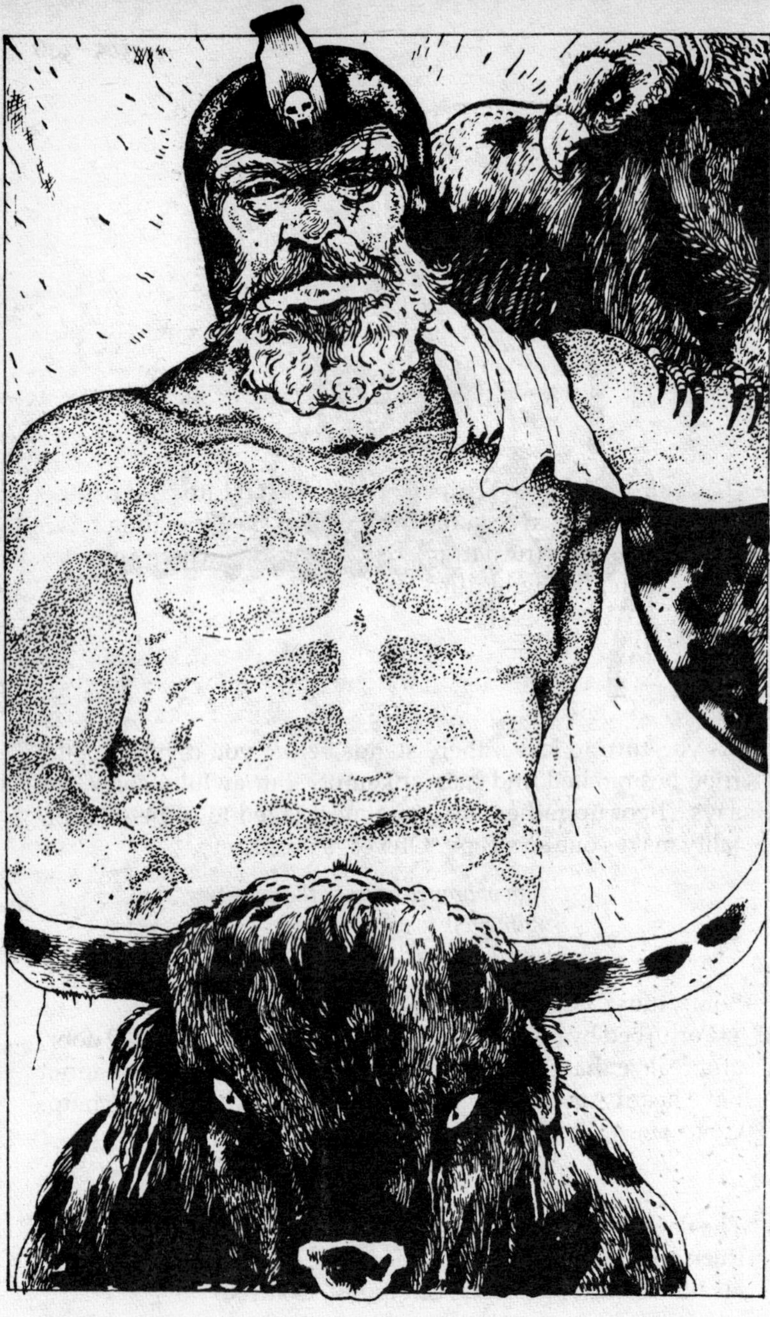

307

Ares the man-crusher seems to stand behind the animal. 'Altheus,' he says, 'be strong. Kill the bull.'

For this combat only, your Might is considered to be 2 points higher than normal. Go to **136**.

308

The priest accepts the gem without speaking, and conducts you to a place in front of the sanctuary. If you were in Disfavour with Apollo, he is now Neutral to you. Go to **181**.

309

The journey to Tiryns is uneventful, and the path clear of other travellers. You arrive in the high-walled city by nightfall. Will you look around (turn to **45**), or look for somewhere appropriate to spend the night (turn to **200**)?

310

You accompany the king to the throne-room, where the lords of the city cheer you, who have saved their monarch. The feasting goes on for hours, and at the end, before you leave, the king's daughter herself bathes you and ritually cleanses your feet. The king fills a wineskin for your journey, and gives to you as a gift a finely crafted mirror, work of a far-off Phoenician master, gilded and inlaid with precious gems. You dress and, collecting your weapons, take your leave of white-walled Thebes. Go to **134**.

311

Have 3 Shame points. Artemis is not your patron. Go to **265**.

312

'Desist from this foul stoning,' you cry, but the Athenians take no notice and your words are lost like pebbles cast into the deep ocean. You see that you can do no good and, averting your eyes from the gory scene, you pass on. Go to **394**.

313

You reach the gate of the palace and knock. The echoes of the blow resound and fill the tiny forecourt with a strange, low moaning. At length an armour-clad guard answers. You tell him your story. He looks sceptical, but beckons you to enter. He disarms you, and searches you for other weapons, which he places on a table near the doorway. These will be returned to you on leaving.

You are conducted along a great hallway, hung with tapestries depicting the triumphs of the gods over the Titans. At length you reach the main hall, where the king himself is seated. The guard pushes you to the ground in front of his monarch, a large, fat, fair-haired man, dressed in a rich but grease-stained robe.

The king sneers, and demands to know what sport has been prepared for today. When he hears your story, he laughs and looks bored. At last he speaks: 'Where are these men? What did you do with them?'

If you allowed the men to go, turn to **274**.

If you killed them, turn to **566**.

314

You have dropped the jewel; this is what made the splash. You feel around and, after a time, you find it and put it back in the pocket of your tunic. You continue on to the town of Cleonae and find an inn. Go to **266**.

315

Take 2 Shame points for killing a host, even one so evil; but have 4 Honour points, and you may keep the axe (Might 5, Protection – 3). You leave the town. Go to **263**.

316

You pick the woman up and carry her into the water. The current is strong, but you find yourself pushing ahead quickly against it. Soon you are approaching the other bank, and the crone speaks, but her appearance is altered, and now you recognize her as Hera, the divine queen.

'Altheus,' she cries above the rush of the water, 'you have done well. Although you did not recognize me, you have done me a favour.' If Hera is your patron, go to **584**. Otherwise, go to **60**.

317

You realize that the priest is waiting for a gift for Apollo. If you have the statuette, and wish to offer it, turn to **554**. If you wish to offer your mother's gem, turn to **308**. If you offer him money, turn to **480**. If you choose not to offer him any of these, go to **43**.

318

You could plunge into the water to fight with the beast in the chill depths of Ocean (**361**). Or you could stand your ground and await its onslaught on the strong-built pines of Aegeus' ship (**484**).

319

No sooner has winged thought escaped your mind than the squall begins to blow once more. Foolish it is, while riding on the waves, to anger Poseidon. Go to **125**.

320

You run quickly away from the camp of the Amazons, fearful lest anyone should spot you and take you prisoner. You must warn Athens of the great host you have seen assembled so close, and tomorrow you must be ready to defend your father's city. Once in the town you reach the white-walled palace quickly, pass through the flower-girt entrance, and explain everything to your father.

Do you stay awake, in case the assault comes at night (**497**)?

Or do you sleep, that you may be refreshed for the coming of life-crushing war (**52**)?

321

As you approach a tight bend, a small boy in the crowd throws a pebble. Your horse shies away and your wheel catches the wall. You are thrown off at the feet of the crowd, but are virtually unharmed. You look around for the boy, but in vain: he is gone. Have 1 Shame point, and lose 2 Honour points. You return, shaken, to the inn, where you rest your aching limbs for the night, not even waiting for the victory celebrations, and ashamed to show your face. In the morning you eat a miserable breakfast, and carry on to Athens (go to **474**).

322

You feel your armour dragging you down towards the bottom. You try to throw it off but it is too late. The monster has you trapped, and yours will be a watery grave, unless you can pray to Zeus. If so, turn to **579**.

323

Away from the island of Melos you sail, the oarsmen straining in their places, for there is no wind. The journey to Thera will be hard, and you lie for a day and a night in your hammock, wracked by some strange fever. In your dreams, sent, perhaps, from Olympus, all the folk you have met glide strangely past. Aegeus, Medea, the captain, your patron, all merging into the hideous laughing face of the Minotaur.

You dash aloft, your fever broken, only to see the isle of Thera lying in the distance, its cliffs reflecting the sunlight like a jewel and casting an unearthly glow. Go to **295**.

324
As you trudge along the dusty road, the midday sun beats down on your back. You sit down to take a drink, and as you do, you notice something strange beside the road. You stand up, and when you reach the place, there is a skeleton, sheathed in rotting leather armour. Across the road a boot and a broken, rusty sword hilt lie, in evidence of an ancient struggle for the traveller's life. The place is overgrown with bushes and scrub. You sigh and utter a quick prayer to your patron that your fate will be a happier one, and that amicable Altheus will live at least to see the halls of his father. But the journey beckons and you set off again to Epidaurus. Go to **277**.

325
Before you can reply, the divine lady has vanished. You make your way through the streets, deserted now in the late-afternoon sun, towards the Acropolis, Athens' citadel, tower-

326

Have 1 Honour point for your decision. It is now nearly dark, and the last glints of the sun's rays die in the west as you reach the harbour. To your horror, when you get to the place where the strong-keeled ship is tied up, you find that your documents for Minos are gone. There is no time to look for them, as the ship must leave at once. Misgiving deep in your heart, you must abandon the letters. Go to **475**.

ing high over the city, as a strong-armed king over his people, their strength and protector. The heat is oppressive and you rest several times, leaning against one of the humble dwellings which make up this part of Athena's town. Go to **244**.

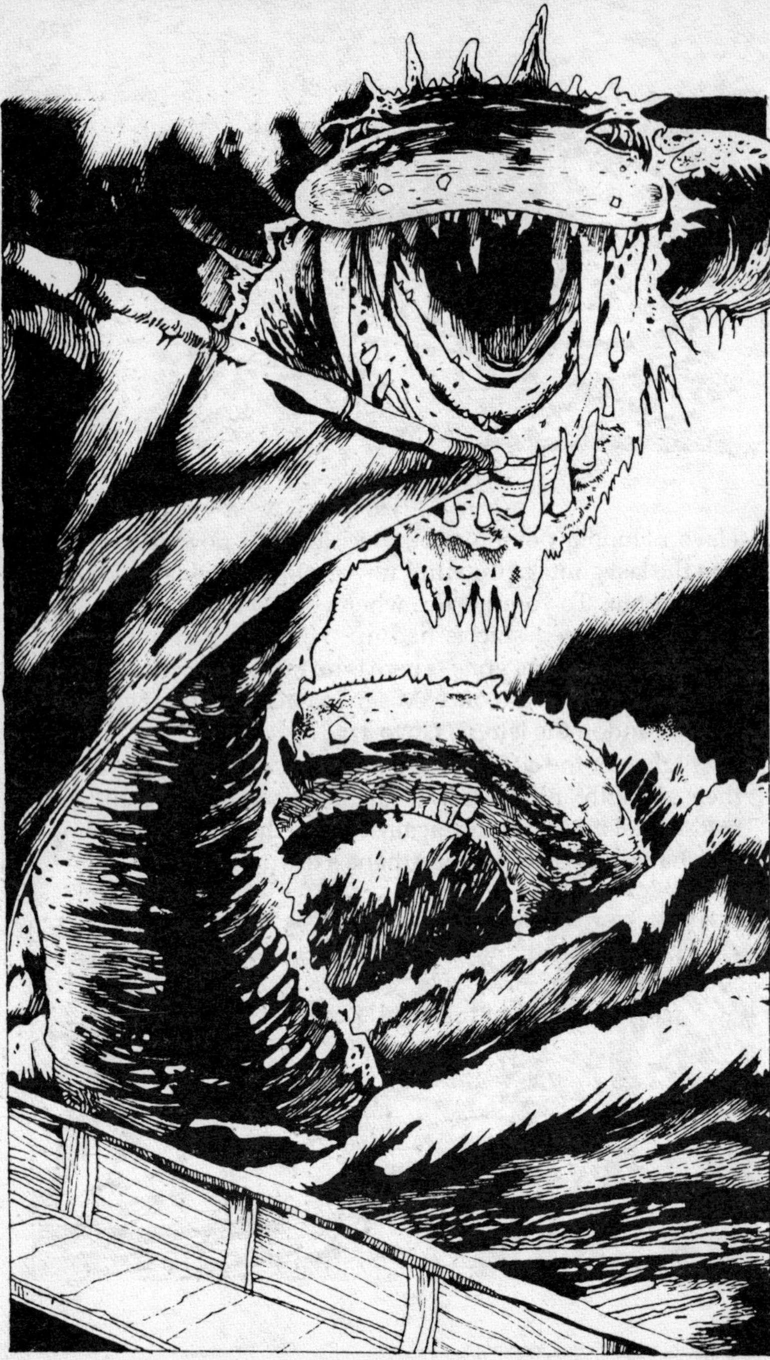

327

The ship has already cast off and the rowers are at their benches, heaving hard at the smooth wooden oars. The overseer has no whip, for all are volunteers, but a regular beat is struck on stretched-hide drums. The Athenians destined for sacrifice speak little, keeping to themselves, but every so often cast you hopeful glances, as men appealing to high Olympus for succour. 'Altheus, breaker of horses, will save us,' they say, or 'Altheus will storm the great-walled citadel of Knossos, and bring us back to Athens.' One girl looks remarkably like your mother Aethra, and puts you in mind for a moment of the home you left so many days ago.

The voyage continues, and the sun and moon take their turns at lighting up the weary world. Sometimes the ship goes under sail; at other times oars are needed. You are seasick often, as the swell rocks the boat, and so unable to help in the necessary tasks of the journey. Your stomach feels as if trampled by the Marathonian bull; your head reels as if being caught a glancing blow by a straight-flying spear. You are dimly aware that the ship, having hugged the coast of Attica, now approaches rugged Ceos. There are shouts and noises above.

'Altheus,' you hear the captain cry, 'come quickly!' You stagger to your feet, and lurch unsteadily to the deck, wondering at the ways of seafaring folk.

When you look out to where everyone is pointing, you see – and horror grips your mind – a great sea-monster, shaped like a serpent, with slimy spines sticking from its head, huge beyond imagining, eyes sparkling with the glint of the deeps, jaws wide and ravening, its body shining blue, green and yellow under the summer sun.

If Poseidon is your patron, go to **448**.

If you are in Disfavour with Poseidon, go to **179**.

If Poseidon is Neutral towards you, go to **577**.

If you are in Favour with Poseidon, go to **547**.

328

'I am amicable Altheus, son of Aegeus,' you retort, trying to put on your most regal voice. The guard looks surprised, but then he beckons you to follow him. You go down a narrow hallway for some time, and then the man gestures for you to enter a room on your left. You go in, realize something is wrong and whirl around – but too late. A cell door is slammed in your face and you are shut in. You turn and survey your bleak prison – no furniture, and rushes on the floor. As the guard leaves, he shouts, 'That's what you get for pretending to be a king's son!' Go to **185**.

329

In the shadows of the murk-filled glade, you see another figure, as you start to unfasten the hairpin from your belt to demonstrate your peaceful intent; it is Ares, god of war, urging you on to the frenzy of the fight.

Either attack the Amazon (turn to **517**) or lose 2 Honour points and turn to **445**.

330

Lose 1 Honour point and gain 1 Shame point for looking! Go to **134**.

331

You eventually find a place to spend the night. It is a pleasant enough inn, almost like the one at Troezen, and the old men quaffing their ale in the corner remind you of the elders of your home town. A sense of homesickness wells up inside you, and you are almost brought to tears by the thought of the house you have left behind. 'Why?' you ask, but you already know the answer; the gods have ordained that you fulfil the task at which your brother died, just as the acorn must strive to become an oak. In the morning, your mind once more at rest, you carry on with your journey.

Your doubts allayed, you may travel to Delphi via Pagae (go to **302**), or to Crommyon (go to **189**).

332
Have 1 Shame point and go back to 312.

333
The bandits have Might 4 and Protection 10. They are both armed with long knives (Might 2, Protection 0). They have no armour. Remember that the first will fight as Might 7: 4 plus 2 for his knife, and 1 for having one companion. The second fights as Might 6 only.

If they are both Seriously Wounded, go to 171.
If you surrender, go to 374.
If you are killed and Zeus saves you, go to 553.
If you retreat, go to 228.

334
You stand outside a huge pigsty. The swineherd is feeding the animals their meal of swill, and he looks up at you inquiringly. The smell is almost overpowering. Do you conquer your disgust and desire to walk away long enough to ask the way to the palace (209)? Or do you leave this place as quickly as possible, and try to make your own way to your father's house (90)?

335
Death and fate close in upon you, but Zeus the almighty turns aside their fearful coming, and instils you with new life. 'Altheus,' you think you hear him say with silent words, 'in exchange for liberation from your death, you must free the people of Marathon from theirs.'

You can carry on the fight. If you win, turn to 282. If you want to retreat, turn to 515.

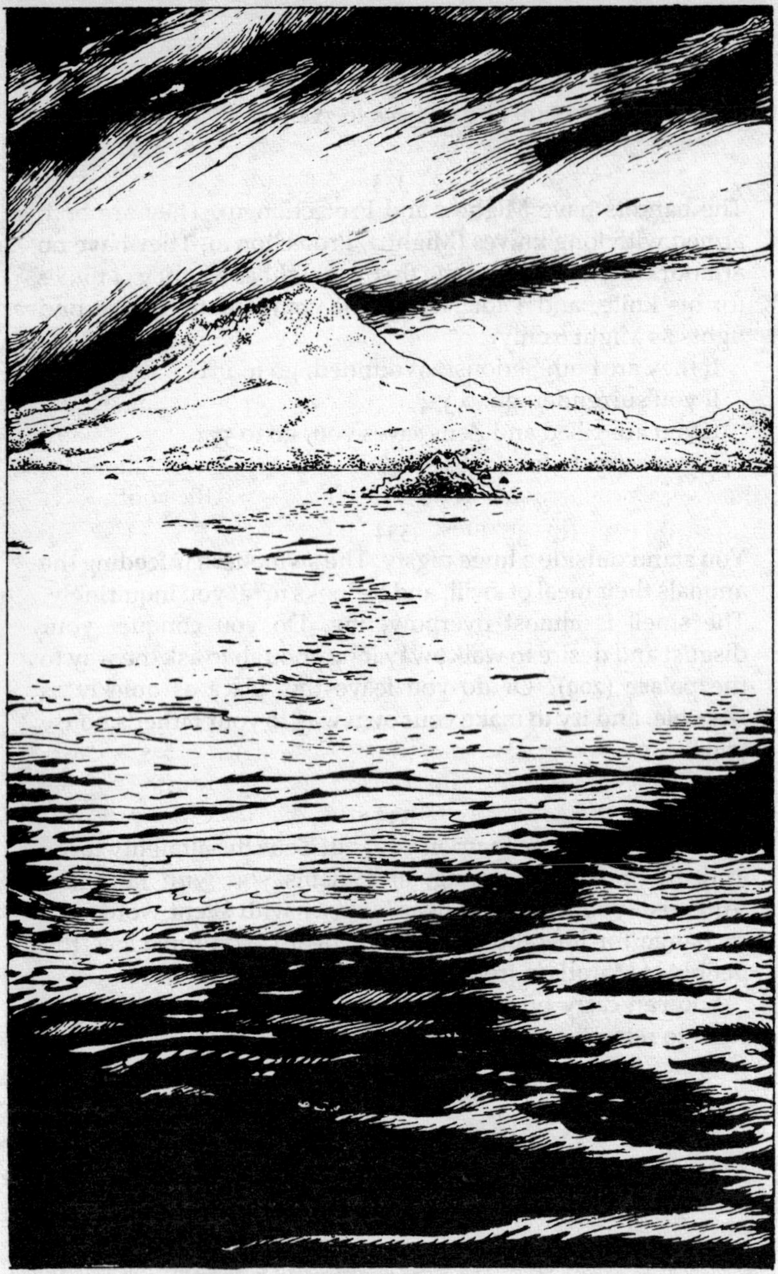

336

One of the sailors shouts, and the others take up the cry. You rush to the bow, and then even you, amicable Altheus, can see it: no longer just a word to you, Crete in all her savage beauty fills the horizon. The seven youths and seven maidens stand in silence, apprehensive of their fate, and you, Altheus, are not immune from the chill hand clutching at their hearts. You have come far and traversed lands that few who are not heroes would have dared. You think of your mother Aethra so far away in Troezen, whom you left so long ago. Your trials have been many: the journey to Athens, the war against the Amazons, the voyage, the sea-serpent, Thera, Cythera and, most recent of all, the grim, high-towering Talos, killer of all things mortal, crusher of beauty, scourge of Attic youth. Your journey is over; your quest has just begun.

The adventure continues in **At the Court of King Minos**.

337

Sweating and trembling at the terrible experience you have just undergone, you open your eyes, only to find that you are still in your bed-chamber. Could this be a message from the gods – a dream sent from high Olympus, or perhaps from the dark depths of Hades? You rise and don your armour, for it is now dawn, and crimson trails light up the early-morning sky. It is time for you to set off for the Piraeus. You stay only a short time to say farewell to Aegeus, and, documents in hand, you set forth on the final stage of your journey to Crete. At the gate the guards salute you, but after a while you become lost, and have to ask a peasant the way to the harbour. Go to **142**.

338

The ship moves towards a headland, hurled on by vengeful Boreas, the north wind. Just as the boat seems it must break against the rocks, the waters part, and from its depths rises Poseidon, lord of the waves.

'Be still!' he cries, and with one swift motion of his trident the sea is calm again, and Boreas banished back to his Thracian cave, just as the assembly is calmed by the wise and soothing words of an experienced speaker, and the trouble-maker is cast out. Poseidon pushes the ship back from the rocks with his mighty hand. With one last wave of greeting, he launches himself back to his coral palace. Go to **194**.

339

In the dim light of dusk, you see a small number of pilgrims at one side of the road, in conversation with a large group of men carrying what look like iron-shafted javelins. The pilgrims seem to hand something over and then carry on their way. As you come closer to the spot one of the men bars your way.

'Halt, pilgrim!' he shouts. 'You must pay for your passage in coin or labour.' He explains that, to get past through Cirrha to Delphi, you must either pay or must plough a certain amount of the field behind, first catching the bull.

Do you submit and agree to pay the money (go to **105**), try to fight the men (go to **264**), or agree to yoke the bull and plough the field (go to **413**)?

340

'Ah, food!' cries the old man, licking his fingers with delight. 'Just as the ambrosia that sustains the high Olympian gods –' he seizes the proffered cheese '– which creates in their veins ichor, the life-blood of the divine ones. Yet from their feet the blood may flow.' Before you can ask what he might mean, he is gone, back to whatever hovel he inhabits. Have 1 Honour point and go to **583**.

341

Leaving the tavern behind, you wander around the town, searching for a more respectable place to stay the night. You find several hostels, but they seem to be full. Eventually you are forced to realize that you will either have to return to the first tavern (go to **36**) or you must sleep in the street (go to **255**).

342

As suddenly as the sun god Helios departs the round of heaven and returns to his graceful home, the storm abates and the winds blow no more. The god of the deeps has been merciful.

Do you offer a prayer of thanks and lose 1 Honour point (**524**)?

Or do you trust that your virtue has been great enough to merit your rescue (**319**)?

343
You make good your escape, but hear the Amazon shouting after you. 'Vile coward! Are all the men of Athens such as you?' Take 1 Shame point and go to **320**.

344
Just as you are about to leave, you notice something glint in the bushes. You investigate. It is an old, rusty helmet, but still useful (Protection 2, Might 0). Pleased with your find, you continue (go to **277**).

345
What is there to fear from warmth and light, amicable Altheus? Zeus smiles upon you, and you quake. For this, lose 1 Honour point. Go to **244**.

346
Have 1 Shame point for your gluttony and your shameful theft. It would be wise to leave Megara at once and carry on to Eleusis. Go to **86**.

347

As you go down the stairs, you see the innkeeper. He sees the blood on your hands, and at once realizes that the unwelcome guests are dead.

'Friend,' he says, 'you are welcome here. You have slain two of the evil brigands who terrorize our town. Yet four more remain. I beg of you to free our temple. Know that the god's gratitude goes with you. I am sure you will not desert us, and I have one small piece of advice. Beware of the trees which line the road to the temple. Ambushers could easily lie hidden within them.'

If you choose to deliver the temple from its evil persecutors, go to 508.

If you do not choose to do so, go to 228.

348

The weather suddenly becomes rougher and the sky darkens over. There will be a terrible storm soon, and you are nowhere near a suitable port. The storm continues to gather. The ship is buffeted by winds and waves. The salt foam crashes over the ship, and you are nearly flung overboard. Beneath you the ship creaks, and the captain tries desperately to haul down the sails. Too late. One of the sailors falls into the sea, screaming horribly, and a gust of wind rips the sail asunder. If Poseidon is your patron, go to 338. If not, go to 393.

349

For the next day and night the ship is driven by a great heaven-sent storm through the deep running waters of Ocean, and its timbers are broken. Three oarsmen are cast into the black whirlpools, never to return to the world of mortal men. Of this you see little, Altheus, for you are too ill. Perhaps your passage would have been eased if Hermes the messenger had granted you the use of his feathered wings to fly to fair Crete.

At last the ship, battered by storm and serpent, arrives at Cythnos for repairs and to take on fresh water to slake the thirst of the tired seamen. You emerge on to the deck, but are carried down the gangway to the harbour, while the crowds look on at this strange ship from Athens. You slump down beside a pile of well-woven baskets, and an old woman revives you with a bunch of grapes.

Do you accompany the captain around Cythnos (**408**)?

Do you explore on your own, moving boldly into the interior (**432**)?

Or do you stay at the quayside, while the fast-moving ship is repaired (**611**)?

350

You soon arrive at the king's great hall. At one end of a vast table Aegeus himself is seated, his nobles beside him. You are honoured with a seat comparatively near the king, and are soon indulging in the best meal you have had since Troezen. There is the meat of deer, duck and boar, the wine-goblets are freely replenished from the mixing-bowl, and there are vast quantities of bread. From a brazier beside the door smoke rises through a hole in the roof, evidence of the burnt remains of a portion of the feast set aside for Athena, the city's patron. Your goblet has not yet been filled with the deep-red wine of Chios' vineyards.

Do you carry on with the meal and wait (**561**)?

Or do you fill the goblet yourself from the mixing-bowl (**85**)?

351

'You have passed our test,' says one of the men, 'for the wine was drugged.' With this he gives it to a passing blind beggar, who drinks it up eagerly.

The men begin to explain their plans. You will be the assassin. You must steal into the king's bedroom through a door that will be left open by one of the guards. There you must kill him while he sleeps. Go to **281**.

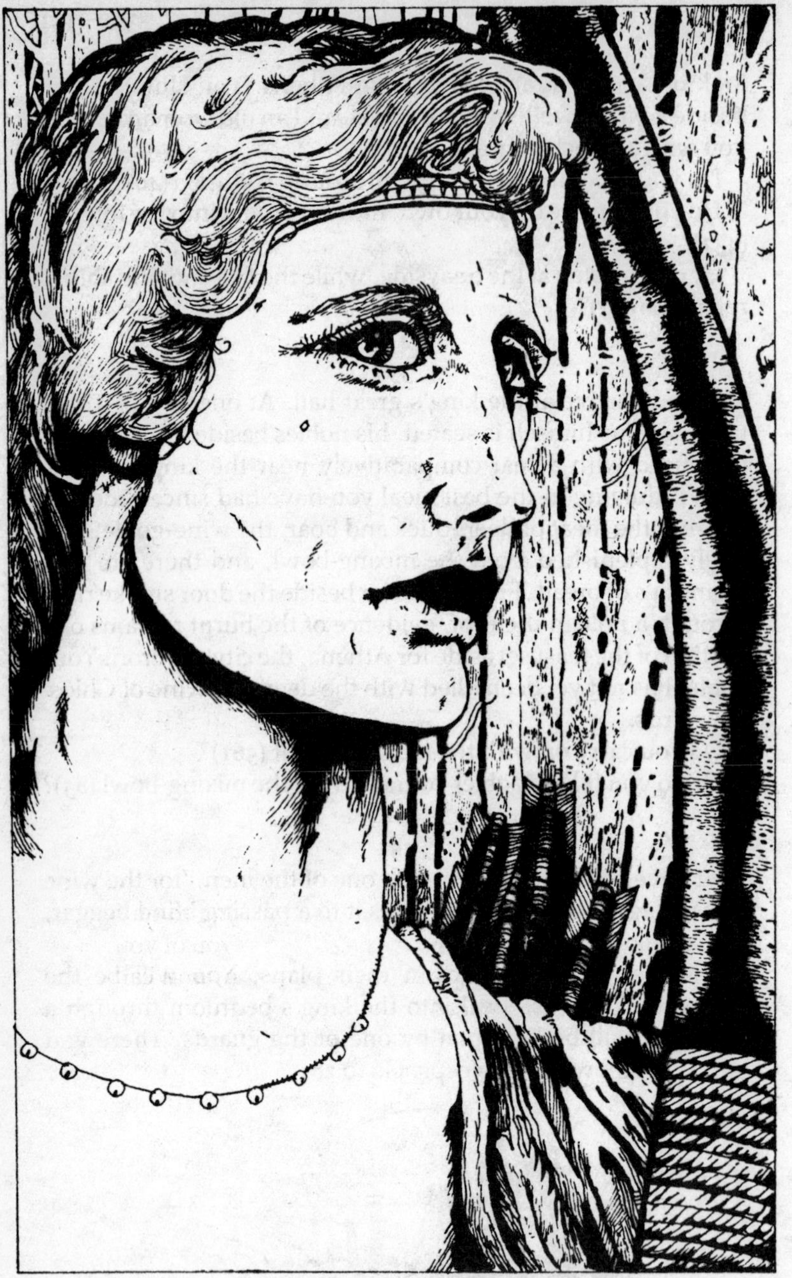

352

In a burst of sunlit glory, the archer god is at your side. 'Altheus. Well, I'm flattered. Take care of yourself: there are lots of problems ahead. I'm going hunting with my sister now, but I leave you my power.' He spits into your eyes, and you can feel the gift of prophecy come upon you. Then the god is gone, as swiftly as he came. You set out for Athens, where your father is king: whenever you take a hint and look twenty paragraphs ahead, ignore any penalty for a non-existent hint. Go to 2.

353

This Amazon is Might 7, Protection 13.
   If you die, and are saved by Zeus, turn to **180**.
   If you retreat, turn to **275**.
   If you surrender, turn to **355**.
   If you Seriously Wound the Amazon, turn to **291**.

354

The men tell you to leave them alone or they will kill you. One of them insults your mother for producing such a dim-witted interfering son.
   Do you attack them for this slur (**37**)?
   Or do you simply leave the inn (**69**)?

355

The Amazon, with a group of Athenians closing in on her, is too hard pressed to do anything except divest you of your best weapon. You are rescued by your companion, and can fight on. Return to **102**, and choose another opponent.

356

You take the water urn and pour its contents on to the brazier. Even the thick smoke cannot hide the joy of the crowd as they celebrate the fulfilment of the springtide mysteries of Eleusis. There are cheers and shouts of joy, as the mantle of winter is cast off. Go to **300**.

357
It is not good to question the motives of the gods. Have 1 Shame point. Go to **142**.

358
To Melos, the fair honey-isle, you travel, and the sea is placid, calm as the tree-tops on a summer's day, when the wind does not blow. No sea-monsters from Poseidon's realm trouble you, and in two days the ship has reached the isle. The sailors disembark, and even those destined for death in the labyrinth seem strangely cheered. Herds of brown-speckled cattle graze in the grassy fields, and birds wheel overhead. Vines grow wild in the countryside, and the sun is warming but not hot.

Do you eat some of the grapes (**586**)?

Do you search for some honey (**276**)?

Or do you join in with the other sailors to try to catch and kill a cow (**59**)?

359
You call on Apollo for aid against these men desecrating the plain. If you are in Disfavour with him, go back to **339**. Otherwise, go to **11**.

360
Apollo is now Favourable to you. Wondering at the manner in which the creature of Hades met his destiny, you accompany the elders back to the ship. Go to **449**.

361
Into the water you plunge, and make for the serpent. From under the water you see that the beast has a soft belly (Protection 6). This will make an easier target. As you struggle to right yourself, however, the snake deals you a great blow to the chest. Blood clouds your eyes, and the water darkens beneath you. You manage to recover in time, but you are now Wounded. Go to **322**.

362

You gasp a prayer to Zeus, and to your amazement see that the bear has gone; it clearly believes you are dead. You lie motionless for almost an hour, fearful lest the creature return. You return to the road, which curves gently to the right. At length it joins another. Go to **13**.

363

For seven days and seven nights the storm rages, and you are blown hopelessly off course. Without rest, the captain strives to keep his ship afloat. The wood of the prow splinters, and is gone. The chest containing Aegeus' gifts to Minos – statuettes of the gods, carved in gold and silver – is swept overboard. Only the will of Zeus keeps the vessel above the whirling waters, while the minions of Poseidon do their best to batter it. You remain below decks, no good sailor, your very life seeming to seep away, as the ship rises and falls.

At long last, when you had almost forgotten that great Ocean, Poseidon's realm, had bounds, the cry goes up that land is in sight, and it is Cythera, Aphrodite's island. Go to **578**.

364

A few seconds pass. Your father returns and leads you by the arm into the doorway, past a plain, unfurnished room through to a tiny study, with a chair and table, on which lies a scroll, ink and writing implements. Have 1 Shame point for disobeying your father. Go to **155**.

365

Each time you try to prise the ichor passage open, seeking to rob the giant's body of its sustaining fluid, you succeed on 4, 5 or 6 (on a roll of one die). For every 5 Honour points spent before the roll, add 1 to it.

If you fail, the giant attacks, and you must return to **48**.

If you succeed, turn to **540**.

366

Your opponent sees that you are the superior fighter, and grips your knees in the traditional gesture of supplication and surrender. 'I am Antiope, queen of the Amazons,' she says. 'You have bested me, and so our nation is defeated. Hera can ask no more. Yet you are a brave fighter, and perhaps you deserve a reward, for you are the first man to best this Amazon queen in mortal combat. There are some of us in Crete, Altheus – for I know of your name and mission – and chief among them is one called Lembra. Speak to her of what you have done, and mention my name. She will be obliged to help you.'

If you kill Antiope now she has told you everything, turn to **454**.

If you let her go, turn to **529**.

367

Bare of all weapons, you go into the camp of your enemy, proud that you will prevent such bloodshed. At the very moment you step among the glowing fires of the gathered host, you feel a sharp pain in your back. You have been stabbed with a strong-shafted spear. Your life-blood flows freely, and Altheus' short span upon the weary earth is done, unless you can pray to Zeus to heal you. If you can, then you may crawl unnoticed back to Athens and arm for the battle. Go to **102**.

368

You grope around, as a man blinded at the hour of glorious victory, for whom there is no sight of loved ones on his return, and all until his life's undoing is dark. Yet you are amazed when your hand touches one of the seals. These are your documents: here is your father's signet imprint in wax. The captain must have handed these over by accident! Without them your time in Crete would have been doom-laden before its start. Thankful in your heart, but with 1 Shame point for your prying, you may either examine the other table (go to **614**), or return straightway to the ship (go to **575**).

369

The rats, squealing in defiance against the invader of their territory, attack you. They will fight as a pack with Might 3, Protection 15.

If you retreat, go to **490**.

If you are killed, and saved by Zeus, go to **51**.

If you are victorious and have not been wounded, have 4 Honour points and go to **213**.

If you are victorious and have been wounded, go to **451**.

370

Surely the visage of your father Aegeus cannot frighten you. Take 1 Shame point, and lose 1 Honour point. Turn to **561**.

371

The creature seems indeed to mean you no harm. It simply circles your vessel, occasionally diving to scoop up some large fish in its cavernous jaws. At last it loses interest and swims off to whatever great cave serves as its lair. Go to **349**.

372

You walk up to the table where the two men are seated. They look up at you questioningly, clearly not pleased at your interruption.

Do you draw your sword and attack them (**37**)?

Or do you try to persuade them not to kill the king of Thebes (**542**)?

373

The cow-eyed queen sends a thought winging on its way from the snow-capped peaks of the gods' palaces down to earth and you, amicable Altheus. At once you realize why the Amazons are attacking Athens: it is because a hairpin sacred to Hera was stolen in a raid by Athenian privateers, and it must be recovered to save Queen Antiope's honour. You must tell Aegeus. Go to **108**.

374

The bandits strip you of your weapons and armour and hurl you out into a field, bound and gagged. Take 1 Shame point for surrendering and being so ignominiously treated. Go to **536**.

375

Despite her great pain, she does not give up the fight. She cannot hit you and in the next round of combat you kill her. Turn to **527**.

376

The Amazon sees that you have surrendered, and cries out in triumph, like one who has achieved her heart's desire. 'So,' she exults, 'an Athenian surrenders to Queen Antiope of the Amazons.' She removes all your weapons, and conducts you at spear-point to a wooden stake near the Amazonian camp. Here you are manacled. Take 1 extra Shame point. You will have no further influence on the course of the battle, hero though you might be. Go to **150**.

377

You have a mild dose of the plague, and lie feverish and in pain for some days. Your skin is marked with scabs, and men avoid you for a time. You lose 2 Honour points. When at last you recover your senses, Athena, the protectress of the town, appears to you in a vision. Go to **213**.

378

It is now dusk: your incident with the sow has delayed you. When you reach the harbour, you are told that the ship to Athens has left. It seems you must continue for the rest of your journey on foot. You decide to spend the night in Crommyon, and soon find a suitable inn. In the morning, well rested and well fed, you set out once more towards your father's palace.

As you leave the town, you come to a sign. You may take a stone-strewn track up over the hills to Pagae (go to **302**), or you may follow the coastal route down to Megara (go to **161**).

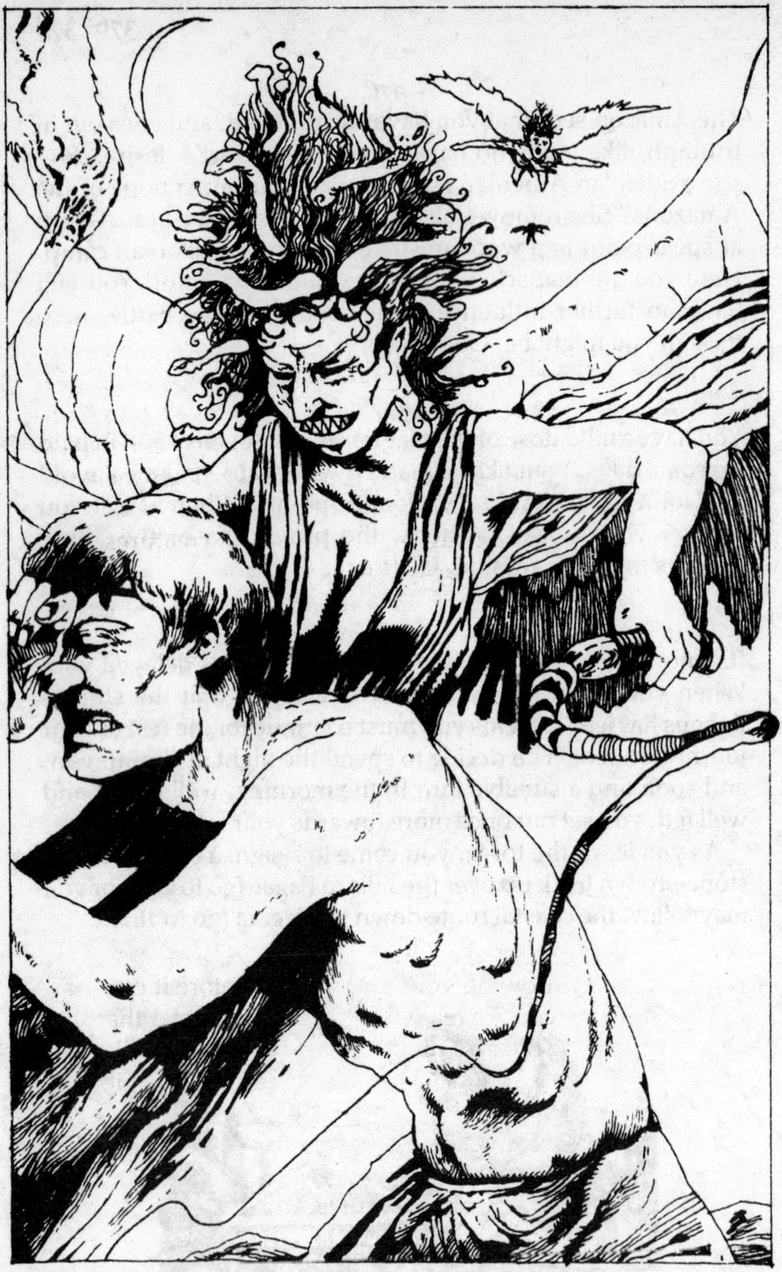

379

The moon is new born tonight, so the way is dark indeed. You stumble often, and once fall down. You rest awhile, and check that your weapons are not broken. The night breeze fills the trees with rustling, and from the branches owls launch silently and lethally upon their prey, scurrying about on the forest floor. In the distance you can now see the lights of the Piraeus, like stars in the realm of heaven. The calm is broken by the voice of a man, pleading for mercy. You move closer, and see a tall young man being set upon by terrible creatures, winged women with snakes in their hair, who tower above him with torches and whips in their hands. In his hand the man holds a cake smeared with honey. Seeing you, he cries, 'Help me! I am persecuted by the Furies. You must help me.'

Do you try to drive away the three winged creatures, and seek the reason for the attack (231)?

Or do you press onwards, thankful that it is not you whom these things have chosen to persecute (473)?

380

The door of the inn is not closed, but inside all is dark. You can make out two tables near the door, on which documents are lying. On one there are sealed papers, while the others are opened.

Do you investigate the opened scrolls first (106)?

Or do you take a look at the sealed parchments (368)?

381

You manage to throw off your armour too, before it can drag you down. Now you are ready to attack this monster that sets upon a harmless ship and rends its meat raw. To it will come vengeance by the hand of Altheus. There is no possibility of retreat.

If you die and are saved by Zeus, turn to 504.

If you Seriously Wound the serpent, turn to 498.

382

An extremely fat woman, who was stirring the contents of a steaming cauldron, notices you and screams for the guards. Within seconds you are surrounded by six of the palace retinue, swords at your throat. It would be best not to resist. Go to **459**.

383

You thank Aegeus cordially for sharing his bread with a stranger in the house, but as you do, you stumble and knock over a goblet filled with wine. It falls to the ground with a resounding clatter, and it seems that every man ceases his chattering and turns inquiringly towards you. Turn to **170**.

384

Leaving the figure of Talos stretched out on the shallow floor of the sea, where he has fallen, you proceed on to Crete. The sun shines dimmer now, partly hidden by clouds of a strange greenish hue. Go to **336**.

385

The queen leaves you, and goes into the fray like a she-bear anxious for her cubs. Within a few minutes, however, the Amazons are in retreat, and like the tide that ebbs from the storm-battered shore, leaving the debris of its coming, they are gone to their far-off haven, their duty to the divine queen fulfilled, their obligation gone. Have 6 Honour points for such a victory, and go to **283**.

386

You spend 2–4 Honour points for Hera's aid (roll a die, divide by 2, round up, and add 1). If you choose to do this, turn to **373**. If you cannot afford Hera's aid, or decide you do not want it now, lose 1 Honour point, and turn to **102**.

387

Headlong to the ship you rush, terrified in your flight from the grim opponent you have faced and not vanquished. Spearfamed Theseus would not have acted so, and allowed such a bandit to ravage the pastures of Troezen. Yet Theseus is dead. The crew hurry in their efforts to provision the ship, while the elders of Delos look on, saddened, still waiting for a hero to come to the isle. You are in Disfavour with Apollo. If he is your patron, go to **596**. Otherwise, go to **492**.

388

You step into the attack. The bandits have basic Might 4, Protection 10, but are armed with greaves (Might 0, Protection 1) and long knives (Might 2, Protection 0), making Might 6, Protection 11 (but Might 7 for the first bandit). They will continue fighting even if Seriously Wounded, fired on by fear of the god. Remember that you may not retreat as the temple is too enclosed.

If you surrender, go to **422**.

If you are victorious, go to **163**.

If you die, and are saved by Zeus, you find yourself, when you recover, at **536**.

389

Darkling anger mars your father's mien for a moment. 'Come now. Speak!' he roars. Mindful of your uncertain position you reply truthfully and say, 'I am Altheus, your son.' Go to **546**.

390

At very peril of your life, you push through the hail of stones to reach the blacksmith. You close your eyes to protect them against the rain of death-dealing dust. When you open them again, the rock-fall has ceased, and the cliff stands black and brooding as ever. The lame man stands smiling, and you can see him more clearly now. He wears a pointed cap, and bears a hammer with which he strokes his great brown beard. His ashen-grey tunic does not cover his right shoulder.

'I greet you,' he booms, his voice like the rumbling of a volcano. 'You have chosen well, and I will reward you.' He turns, and for a moment you see in the rock a great workshop, shining like the stars, with an anvil, and a multitude of bellows, blowing like the great storms that break the hollow ships, and send the crews to their doom. Then, just as swiftly, the scene vanishes. In his arm, he bears a breastplate, shield and sword. He hands them to you, and they shine in the sunlight, like the sun come to earth, plain worked but stronger than death. You take these divine gifts and marvel, but as you do, the god is gone, back to his celestial workshop.

These weapons are divine work, and are therefore mighty indeed. Normally the breastplate is Protection 4, the shield Protection 4, and the sword Might 4, but when fighting divine, or divinely built creatures, all values are at 6, not 4. Such creatures are marked in the text with an asterisk (*) before their Might value.

You are in Favour with Hephaestus. Go to **495**.

391

The race is handled by you, the player. The blue team is number 1, the red team number 2, the yellow team number 3 and the green team number 4. Roll two dice. Each of the numbers rolled, if in the range 1 to 4, shows that that numbered chariot advances one segment of the course. The course is divided into ten segments; the first to complete ten segments is the winner. You should keep a track of how many segments a chariot has completed. If 5 is rolled no one advances. If 6 is rolled, everyone advances one space. If double 6 is rolled, roll one further die, as there has been a chariot crash. If 1–4 is rolled, then that number chariot crashes and is out of the race. A 5 is a near miss, with no chariot actually crashing, while 6 means that all chariots in the race crash, and the contest is over. Note that if double 1, 2, 3 or 4 is rolled, then that chariot may advance two spaces. If there is a tie at the end, the chariots involved continue until one establishes a lead, when it is deemed the winner.

If Poseidon is your patron, or you are in his Favour, go to **44**.
If all the chariots crash, go to **618**.
If the chariot on which you are betting wins, turn to **447**.
If the chariot on which you are betting loses, turn to **427**.

392

The road is tree-lined now, and you think you see satyrs and fauns in the glades, but whenever you investigate they have gone. You carry on, and the milky-white moon filters through the swaying trees. The wind caresses your face, but all else is strangely silent.

Suddenly, out of the bushes a snow-white hart leaps, gazes at you for a moment with frightened eyes, and then bounds into the forest on the opposite of the path.

Ahead the road forks. You could go to the left (**251**) or to the right (**13**).

393

The ship is hurled uncontrollably towards a headland. Jagged rocks emerge evilly from the water, and tear the heart from the pine-built bark. Sailors, screaming, are thrown against the rocks, their life's blood spilling in the black sea, forever lost in the boundless waters. Others fling themselves from the boat, seeking to reach the shore by striving against the wild sea. The ship's figurehead breaks off, and is carried far off to sea. The captain screams incoherently, life already broken by the loss of his ship, and hurls himself into the water.

You can stay with the wreckage of the ship, and hope to be saved (go to **53**).

Or you can jump into the sea and try to swim to the shore (go to **425**).

394

As you walk onwards into the city, a small boy laughs wildly at you. The sky darkens over, and the air becomes hot and heavy. A few spots of rain drop and mingle with the dust on the road. Moments later the path begins to turn to mud, and people take shelter as the rain crashes down. Before you can get to cover you are completely soaked. Away in the distance the thunder rumbles. There is a brilliant flash and the Acropolis is bathed in blue light, and almost at once an ear-splitting clap of thunder seems almost to herald the rending of the sky.

Will you attempt to find shelter near by (**94**)?

Or will you press on to try to find the palace (**186**)?

395

'Well, you have got yourself wet, haven't you?' says the woman, grooming her hair. 'It was a nice thought, though. Goodbye now, and better luck next time, you silly thing.' In the flutter of an eyelash, she has gone, and the realization comes to you all that this was Aphrodite, goddess of beauty. Go to **608**.

396

You pray to your patron god that you might escape this awful plight. With one great heave you manage to uproot the stake, and your chains fall down to the ground. The gods have freed you, but perhaps too late, for the battle's course is nearly run, and the dead lie all around, like towers which have crashed down, from the force of the encounter.

Do you make your way back towards the city (**510**)?

Or do you stay to fight out the closing of the struggle (**597**)?

397

Silently you sit, patiently awaiting the advent of the bull. Suddenly, some way off, you see a large shadow looming in the distance. Stealth learnt in the long years of hunting at Troezen comes to your aid, and you manage to creep up on the bull without its noticing.

Just as you are about to strike, it senses you, and turns round, so that you can see its man-piercing horns, as long as a sword, its huge jaw, and fearful red-rimmed eyes, glowing like coals on a fire.

If Aphrodite, Hera, or Apollo is your patron, turn to **160**.

If Poseidon or Athena is your patron, turn to **136**.

If Ares is your patron, and you desire his aid, turn to **488**; otherwise, turn to **136**.

If you have no patron, turn to **160**.

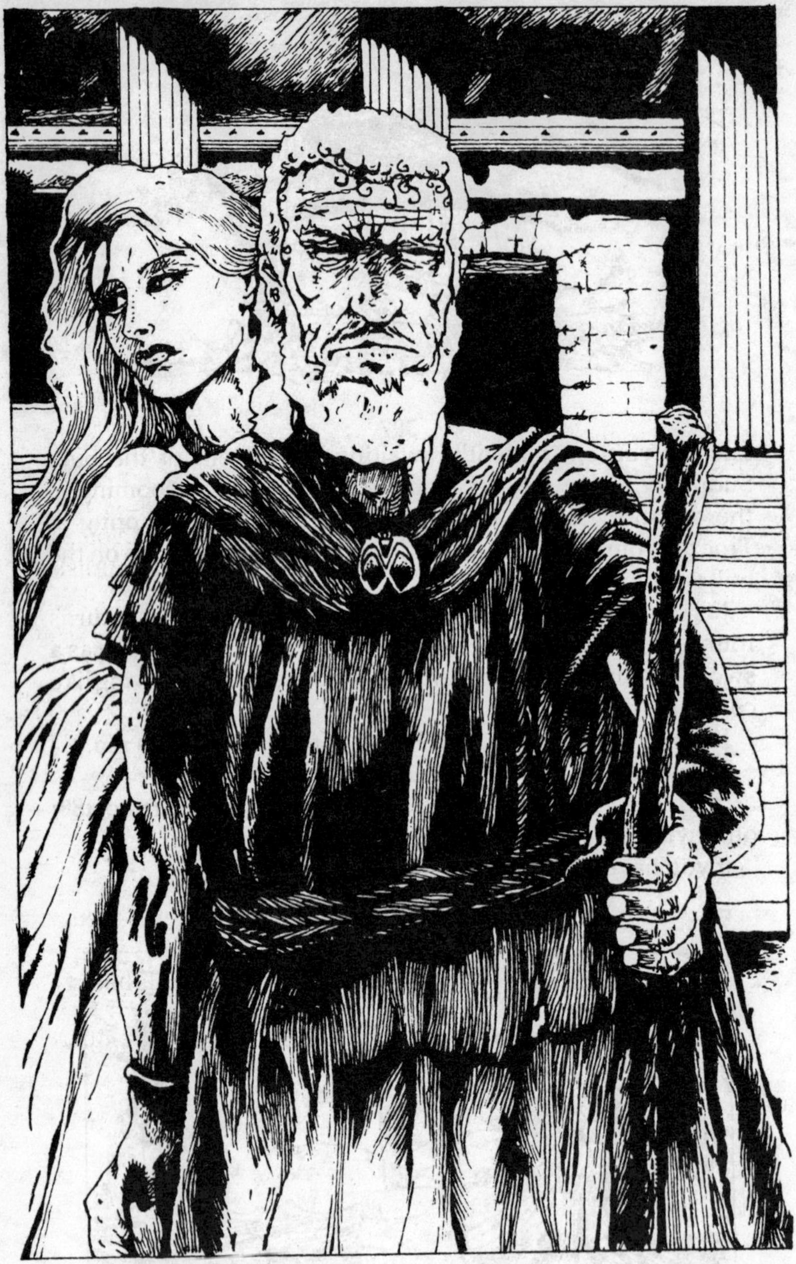

398

You leap up the temple steps. The priests, expecting nothing of the sort, are taken aback. You seize the girl from the aged high priest, and turn to rush away from the temple. One of the crowd bars your way, but you knock him down with a single blow of your fist. The rest are too stunned to react, and you manage to disappear into the gathering crowd before anyone thinks to stop you.

The temple far behind, you pause, breathless. You turn to gaze at your new-found companion. You think to yourself that perhaps she is more beautiful than Aphrodite. Hardly has this thought taken form than the divine lady herself stands at your side.

'There's really no comparison, is there?' she teases. You shake your head in adoration. 'It was terribly nice of you to find me a new handmaiden,' she continues with a girlish giggle. Aphrodite then disappears, taking the girl with her back to her silk-carpeted palace on high Olympus. You are now in Favour with Aphrodite, but in Disfavour with Hera. If Aphrodite is your patron, go to **133**. If not, you leave Megara, and continue on to Eleusis, evading any attempts to capture you. Go to **86**.

399

These creatures are the Furies, Tisiphone, Alecto, and Megaera. They punish those who have committed some heinous crime. To help the man would be to offend them, while to leave him would be shameful indeed.

Do you try to give succour to the man, and beat off his hellish assailants (**231**)?

Or do you decide not to offend these deities of the underworld, and carry on to the ship (**473**)?

400

Have 2 Honour points, and remember that wounds heal. You may then carry on down the path to Epidaurus. Go to **277**.

401

The innkeeper drops to his knees and begs for mercy. You see the snivelling wretch at your feet and, rather than pity, you feel fury at one who has treated you so shamefully.

Do you kill him anyway (turn to **290**), or do you spare his life and spend the night in the inn (go to **564**)?

402

It really would be best not to resist. Take 1 Shame point, and turn to **459**.

403

Have 2 Shame points for killing opponents who have surrendered, but 6 Honour points for having bested them. Go to **347**.

404

You take some of the corn seed from the bowl, and sprinkle it on the brazier. Dark smoke rises as the seed burns. You choke and splutter, but then you see the reaction of the assembled mob. There is a stunned silence. Then, from all sections of the crowd, comes the cry, 'Stone him!' Missiles rain down; people rush up the steps, tear the very armour from your body, and snatch away your weapons. The priestess steps forward and calms the fury of the crowd. 'Stop,' she cries, 'there will be no bloodshed. Let him go, and may Demeter's vengeance find him swiftly.'

You have lost all your weapons and armour, must have 3 Shame points, and are in Disfavour with Demeter.

You rush out of Eleusis before the crowd attacks you again. Go to **138**.

405

'I, your patwon, will twansport you to the Acwopolis, so you may look over my favouwite city. Wemember also that you must show your mother's gem to your father Aegeus. When he asks who you are, then is the time.'

With this the divine lady is gone, and you find yourself on the Acropolis gazing down at the city below. Go to **49**.

406

It is dark and very cold when you reach the river. Your clothes, still wet from your earlier crossing, make you shiver uncontrollably. Still, you realize the importance of the jewel and control your limbs, pushing on into the centre of the stream. When your will to carry on has almost left you, and you would have abandoned your task, you find the gem, and return to the bank. You collapse into a deep sleep, and in the morning, still cold, but less tired, you may carry on past Cleonae. However, for turning back during your quest, and for carelessly losing such an important token, you must have 1 Shame point. Go to **3**.

407

Retreat from such as these is hardly the act of a hero. As you rush headlong into the maze of streets, eventually losing your pursuers, you wonder what your brother Theseus would have done. In addition to the normal penalty for successfully retreating, you must take 1 Shame point. Go to **230**.

408

Quickly you move away from the strong-benched vessels in the harbour, where swift preparations are made for the repair of the ship. The Athenians bound for Crete stand in a forlorn group chattering among themselves, but you leave them behind. At last you catch up with the captain, who is talking to a man outside the inn. He hands over some scrolls of parchment, and then speaks to you with winged words: 'Come in and join me for a drink.'

Do you accept (**243**)?

Or do you decline gracefully and walk on without him (**525**)?

409

As the ship weighs anchor, and you scramble ashore through the shallows, you see that the boat has been thrown against the rocks and torn open. The woman's body lies limp and lifeless on the beach, while the sand runs red.

If Aphrodite is your patron, turn to **278**.

Otherwise, turn to **35**.

410

As you start down the right-hand path, you see a grey wolf creep out of the undergrowth and slink towards you along the dusty road. If you want to take the left-hand fork after all, turn to **499**. If you want to fight the wolf, go to **208**.

411

In the morning you waken, just at the time when fresh Dawn comes and with her crimson streamers lights up the pale sky. Today is clearly the day of the assault. A serving-maid brings you in a hearty meal of meat and goat's milk. Once you have eaten, you go down to meet Aegeus.

He stands, pensive, and in his arms he bears his own weapons and armour. 'This,' he says, 'is all I have left. Much has been lost, and I am too old to use what remains. Go now and save our city from this dire peril, and may the gods be with you.' With this, he hands you a sword (Might 3, Protection 0), a small shield (Might 0, Protection 2) and a breastplate (Might 0, Protection 2). You may use these items in combat if they are better than the arms you already possess.

If you have been told the reason for the Amazon attack on Athens, turn to **548**.

If Hera is your patron and you desire her aid, turn to **386**.

Otherwise you must go and join the fray at once. Go to **102**.

412

You follow the hart into the bushes and you find yourself tiring as the animal darts elusively to and fro ahead of you. Now its speed outstrips your failing limbs entirely, and you fall to the ground to recover. Go to **111**.

413

Defiant, you step towards the bull, trepidation far from your mind. You leap on to the bull's back, clasp its horns and wait for it to toss and try to throw you off, thinking to gore you with its man-piercing horns, as the hunter dispatches his fleet-footed prey with an iron-headed spear. But it does not move, nor even seek to throw you. In fact you find you cannot make this docile bull move, and in the end, to the jeers of the watching people, you are forced to move the plough to the bull. Pride in your heart, you complete the allotted portion of the field, and are on your way quickly, but as you go you hear with horror what the people are shouting. You have ploughed the sacred field of Apollo! Tricked, tormented, and now in Disfavour with the god, you carry on towards Delphi. Go to **92**.

414
The merchant whose stall was being robbed comes up to you and says, 'I am pleased to see that honesty and the code of Honour still prevail. For your service I would like to make you a gift.' He hands over a rather old, but still strong shield. 'This is mine, but I have no use for it any more. Take this shield: I used it once in Crete, though I doubt you've ever been there. All I ask is you don't dishonour it, and remember my name: Cyron.' The shield is Might −1, Protection 3. You continue on your way from Megara to Eleusis, sacred to Demeter. Go to **86**.

415
The innkeeper gasps as he sees you slaying the conspirators, but before he can act you are out of the inn. You rush down a side alley to avoid pursuit, but there is none. Some minutes pass and you feel it is safe to return to the main highway.

Do you go to the palace, and try to warn the king (**313**)?

Or do you leave Thebes as fast as you can (**134**)?

416
At length you reach the temple itself. On the wide white steps there stand the priestesses of the great goddess, chanting and wailing their rite. The crowd is hushed, straining to hear every word, and silent in anticipation of some great event.

Then the high priestess begins to move among the crowd, touching now one, now another, brushing them with her yellow robe, but never satisfied. Her motions become more frenzied, like one inspired by the goddess. At last she comes to you. Gripping you by the upper arm, she draws you up to the temple steps. Go to **248**.

417

Tired and wet, you drag your wearied limbs along the road to Cleonae. It is approaching nightfall. Hunger built up overnight and through the day's journey begins to twist your stomach's base at the thought of inn's fare at Cleonae. You reach the place and knock at the door. A greybeard carrying a lantern answers. You ask for a room, but the man is gruff and shoos you away. He slams the door, carved from triple pine, felled in the mountains above Parnassus of the snowy peaks under autumn's benevolent sun. You reach into your pocket for money, and realize that the jewel is gone. You must have dropped it in the river!

You can knock again, and offer the innkeeper twice the usual price (go to **285**).

You can return to the river to seek the jewel (go to **406**).

Or you can spend the night in the street (go to **23**).

418

'A gift, a gift!' shrieks the wild man with unholy glee, picking small insects out of his beard and squashing them between his fingers. You find that most of your possessions are on the ship, but you could give him some food (go to **340**), a piece of armour (go to **479**) or a weapon (go to **292**). Alternatively, you could give him nothing (go to **253**).

419
Have 1 Shame point and lose 1 Honour point. Return to **399**.

420
You may skin the wolf. Wearing the pelt gives 2 points of Protection, and is imposing enough to give 1 Honour point. Go to **277**.

421
Shame on you, Altheus! For reading this paragraph, to which you cannot have been sent, have 15 Shame points. Go back to where you came from.

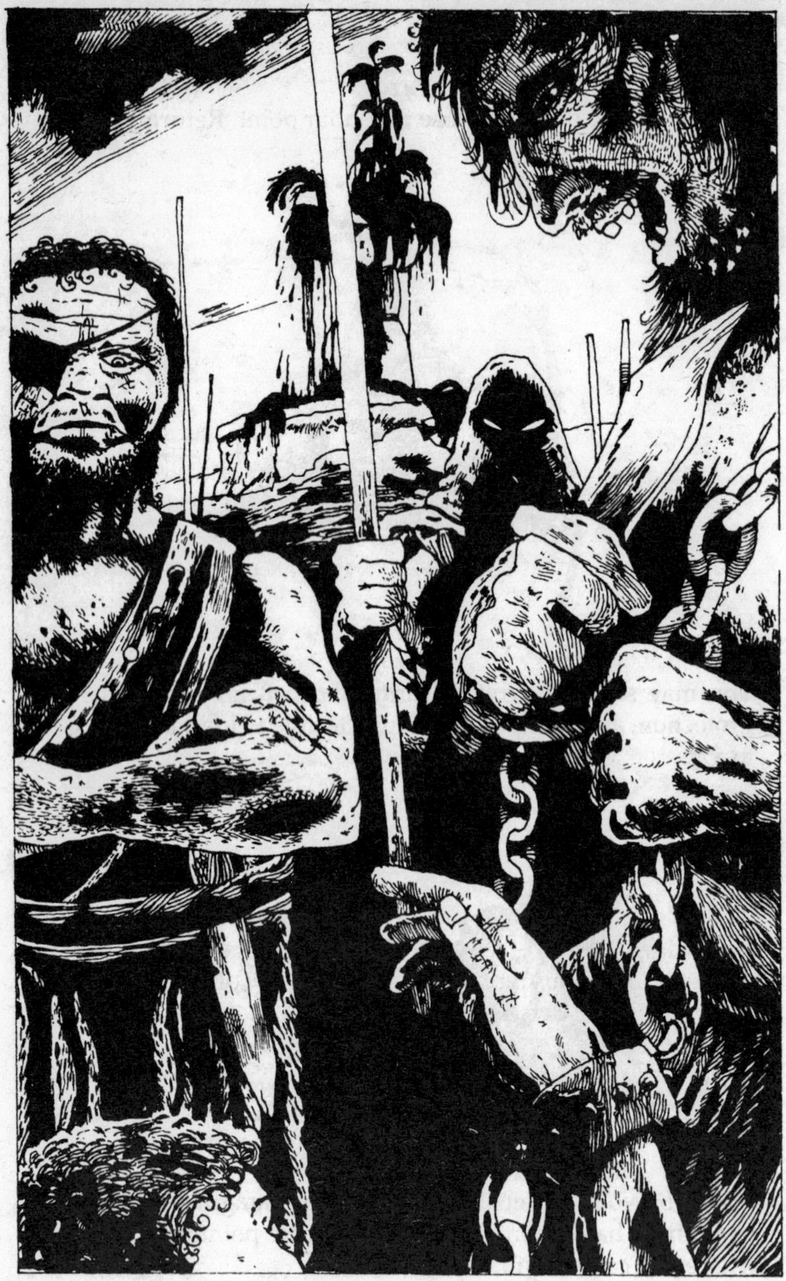

422

Your black-hearted foes seem unwilling to spare you. Your weapons thrown on the ground, they drag you towards the blood-flowing fountain. With a shock you realize they will drown you in the unholy gore.

Do you try to escape (go to **114**)?

Do you allow yourself to be thrown into the fountain (go to **537**)?

Or do you pray for aid to your patron god (go to **250**)?

423

Thankful that you have not spent a miserable night alone in bed, you make your way to the perimeter of the walls, which is the course of the race. As you arrive, the crowd catches sight of the front runners; the red and the green teams' chariots thunder towards you, jockeying for position as they approach a bend in the wall. Without warning, the green chariot cuts inwards, and the red driver is forced to swerve. As he does so his wheel hits a large stone. His chariot bounces and tips over. He struggles frantically to control it, but in vain: it overturns. The driver is dragged along, tangled in the reins for a time before the horse plunges into some spectators. Several people are trampled, but at last one of the charioteers not driving in this race brings it under control. The driver is badly injured, and a small crowd gathers around him. Just as you reach the spot, you hear him gasp out in pain.

He is carried into an inn, and there set down on a table. The landlady bustles over to speak to him, but all he is interested in is who is to take his place in the red team. He offers the chance to drive his spare chariot to whoever bets on the winner in the next race. Three young men bet various large sums of money.

Do you approach him to place a bet on the next race, so that if you win your bet, you can drive in the race after that (go to **207**)?

Or do you just watch the races (go to **9**)?

424

The wind blows into a gale, and the ship is tossed from side to side. The masts are stripped of their black cloth sails, which are thrown into the sea, and then they too are splintered like the stockade before the coming of the angry boar, its mouth foaming, its eyes wild as the stormy seas. The ship is beaten down by the fury of the waves, and all aboard fear for their lives.

You may either sacrifice 2 more Honour points to Poseidon (go to **619**), or you may trust in your own ability to ride out the waves (go to **33**).

425

You take one last glance at the pitiful scene on deck, and dive into the frothing sea. The icy water makes you gasp; a wave breaks over your head. As you struggle to the surface, you see ahead the best swimmers already close to land. Suddenly a mighty crash rings in your ears and behind you the ship, now smashed, slips under the waves. Your tunic has become waterlogged and you find it hard to swim. Your arms are very weary and you feel you can go no further. The cold numbs your body and, still far from the shore, you slide into senselessness. Go to **247**.

426

There are many people rushing around, but no one seems to take any notice of you. An old man sits dejectedly on a large flat stone, staring into the throng of people, as if remembering earlier, better years. Past you there walks a young man, dressed in a rich tunic of purple trimmed in gold, clearly of high birth.

Do you stop the nobleman, and ask him the way to the palace (**514**)?

Or do you approach the old man (**104**)?

427

Disappointed, you return to the wounded charioteer. He is already trying to teach the young nobleman who won the bet how to drive. He, however, simply takes up the whip, and applies it liberally to the horse. It reacts violently and careers off towards you. You manage to bring the animal under control. In the chariot the nobleman looks pale, and decides to forgo the race.

You are immediately offered the chance to drive the red chariot. You accept. Go to **169**.

428

To your horror you notice that the documents destined for Minos at Crete are among the papers. Hurriedly you stop the innkeeper and explain the mistake. He smiles and hands them back. You decide that it would be better to return to the ship, before the malicious barbs of the spirits of Cythnos can wound you further. Go to **575**.

429

Clearly grateful to you for sparing their lives, the men stand, and, somewhat warily, begin their tale. 'You must believe us when we tell you that the king of Thebes is to be killed this night. One of the palace guards has been bribed to leave open a door in the courtyard, that leads to a staircase. From here the assassin will ascend to the king's room, and kill him while gentle sleep has robbed him of his wits. Warn the king, if you will, but say nothing of our part, and all-powerful Zeus will smile on you for the rest of your days.'

Do you let the men go on their way (**518**)?

Or do you kill them, now that they have told you what you need to know (**184**)?

430

Down along the sea's edge you run, and when at last you turn to look, the old man is still standing where you left him, and has not ceased his endless chatter. Your head throbs, and you feel unwell. At length you reach a spot near the ship and there sit for a rest. Go to 583.

431

You fall to the ground, and grasp the knees of your assailant. The woman throws back her head and laughs. 'Know, stranger,' she says, 'that you have surrendered to Hippia. Yet the struggle between our races is for the morrow.' With this she divests you of your best piece of armour and your best weapon, and allows you to go. Remember the 1 Shame point for surrendering, and go to 320.

432

Cythnos is a fair island, not as fair as Salamis in Attica's lovely land, but the houses are well built and the people happy. Even the dogs seem to have life-bringing joy in their hearts. You are offered food, fruit and drink all day long. It is only when dark gloom begins to wrap her tentacles around the earth, and you are in danger of being mazed by her snares, that you return to the harbour. Have 1 Honour point for your *laevendia* throughout the day, and go to 279.

433

You are flung into the storeroom, and hit your head heavily against the stone floor. Bleeding profusely, you lapse into unconsciousness. Later you are awakened roughly, and looking up you see the two men whose lives you spared in the inn. 'Only fools spare their enemies, and we will not make that mistake. The king is dead, and so, amicable Altheus, shall you be in a little while. We followed you, and when we saw you go to the palace, we realized that you had betrayed us. We changed our plan, and caught the king unawares.'

With this one of them unsheathes a large, curved sword, and thrusts it deep into your chest. You hardly have time to pray to Zeus before your spirit wings its way to the fields of Elysium. If you do pray to the divine one, he will revive you, and you find yourself at paragraph **134**.

434

The tale of Herakles is stirring indeed, and you find yourself inspired by the example of the earlier hero. The bard tells of how high-hearted Herakles slew the Hydra with its many heads. At length the story changes, and now he chants of how Daedalus and his son Icarus constructed the great labyrinth of Crete, and, imprisoned by King Minos, escaped and flew from Crete on wings sealed with wax, but Icarus perished, wings melted by the hot sun.

At length you grow tired and resolve to set out once more for the palace (go to **137**).

435

Cautiously you lift the urn to your lips, and take a small sip. You put the urn back on the table, but the crowd still waits expectantly for you to act. You must return to **58**, and choose again.

436

Breaking free of the priestess's grasp, you decline to be involved in the ceremony, saying that you are a stranger. The crowd shrinks away, as if you were infected. You leave the city hurriedly with shouts and cries ringing in your ears. You must have 1 Shame point, and are now in Disfavour with Demeter. Go to **138**.

437

Clearly the reason the innkeeper will not let you stay is that you are still soaking wet from your crossing of the river.

You can dry off and return later to the inn, without going back to the river (go to **266**).

You could return to the river to seek the jewel (go to **406**).

Alternatively, you can insist on spending the night in the inn (turn to **564**).

438

The coward falls at your feet begging for mercy. You kick him away, and he hits his head on the wood of the stall. Still dazed, he is dragged away by the market-wardens, who are clearly grateful for your intervention. Have 2 Honour points and go to **414**.

439

The Furies, it is said, can be appeased by sacrifice of honey, cakes and milk. You realize that this is exactly the meal you have brought with you from Athens to eat on the way to the great-prowed ship for Crete.

Do you attack the unearthly sisters (**231**)?

Or do you try to offer them a sacrifice (**303**)?

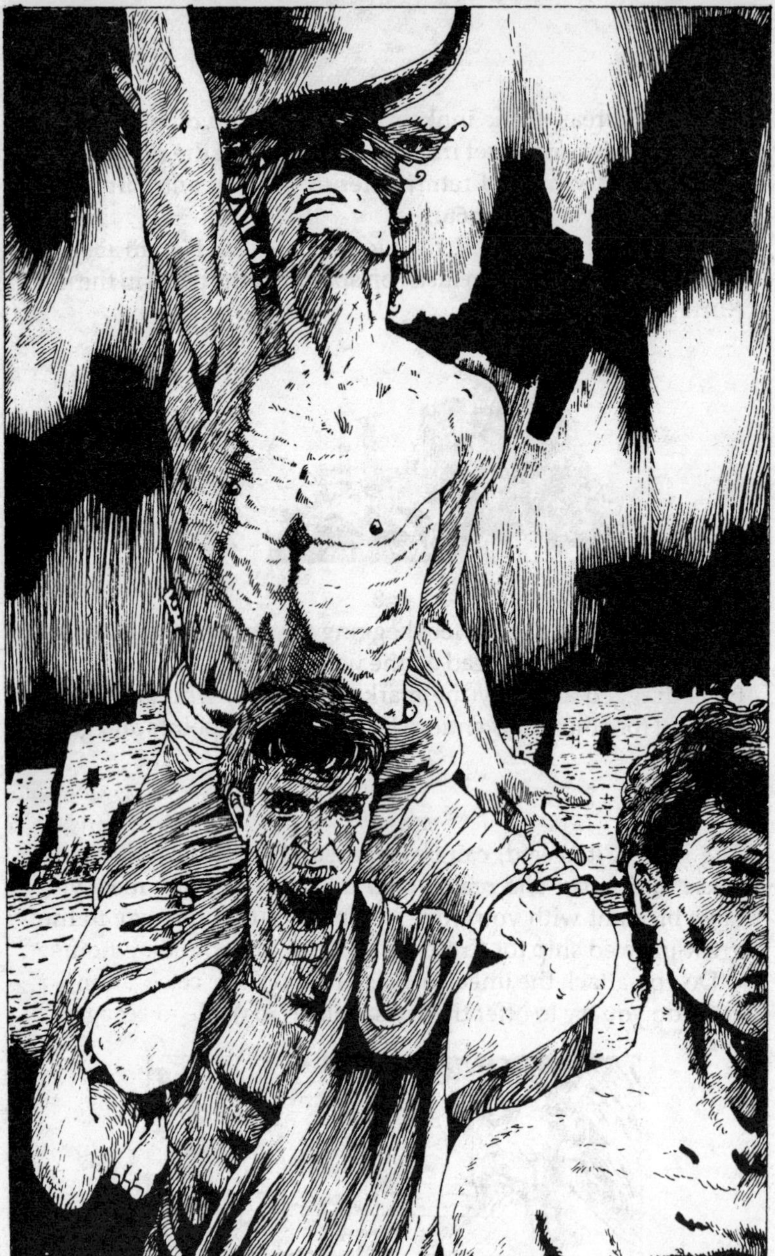

440

You are deep in the heart of the city now. Surely the palace must be somewhere near by. Turning a corner, you suddenly come upon several citizens watching a group of men with whitened faces. You go nearer, and see that they are silently representing some legend. Some pretend to eat, others are drinking imaginary wine. You cannot make out what it is. Then, of a sudden, it becomes clear to you. They are depicting the death of your brother Theseus in the labyrinth. One man climbs on another's back, and is the Minotaur. Another represents Theseus, treading with exaggerated caution through the labyrinth, pausing from time to time to lean on the wall. He bends to pick something up from the ground and the Minotaur attacks him from behind. Theseus mouths a cry of agony, and falls motionless. For a moment the scene freezes; then the Minotaur separates back into two cart-wheeling players, and Theseus springs up from the ground.

You realize with a start that no one could know of your brother's death. You look again at the players, but all save one is vanished. His face is that of Hermes, the divine messenger. He gives one last enigmatic smile, and is gone. Go to 592.

441

You are tired after the exertions of the day, and your youthful limbs can hardly bear you further. You stagger, and fall to the ground. A man comes to you and puts a goblet to your lips, and you sip at the cool dark wine. You are carried by servants of Aegeus to your room, and there you rest for some hours, sleeping intermittently, while the feast and the celebration go on below. At last you are recovered, and feel able to act again, fully refreshed.

Do you stay the night, ready to leave next morning (476)?

Or do you decide that you can delay no longer and must go at once without saying farewell down to the Piraeus, port of Athens, where a ship awaits you, carrying the human tribute for Minos (379)?

442
If Apollo is your patron, turn to **299**. Otherwise go to **18**.

443
You drop your weapons, and spread your arms in a gesture of peace. It is to no avail. One last great rock comes crashing down, splintering and cracking the bark from end to end, and spilling all your lives' bloods into the ever-hungry seas. Your journey is over: eternity has just begun.

444
Before your shameful blow can be struck, wreaking a miserable murder, the old hag's visage suddenly transforms. She is no mere mortal, but proud Hera, queen of the gods. You try to drop to your knees, but it is no good. Divine anger freezes you, as the stag before the hungry lion stays and does not escape its doom.

'I am very disappointed with you, Altheus,' she intones. 'I always thought you were one of the nicer heroes. Well don't come running to me for help in the future because you won't get any.' With this she vanishes. You must take 3 Shame points. If Hera is your patron, she will not aid you (although it is possible for you to get into her Favour again as if she were not your patron – you simply lose all the benefits of patronage and are treated as if you have no patron), otherwise you are in Disfavour with her. Go to **294**.

445

'I am sent by the great King Aegeus as emissary,' you cry, 'so stay your strong-armed blows and conduct me to your queen. I bring with me that sacred gift of Hera upon which our quarrel hinges.' With this you unfasten the hairpin from your belt, and hold it forth. The moon throws down her gentle rays and illumines the glade. The Amazon nods, lowers her spear and beckons for you to accompany her. Soon you are among the multitude of tents; your guide stops at one and motions for you to enter. Turn to **8**.

446

'Get up!' A voice awakens you from slumber. 'Fool,' it continues, 'to come to Epidaurus.' Your eyes grow accustomed to the dark. Now fully awake, you see that two burly men have entered your room and are standing over you. One seizes you by the arm, and hauls you up.

'Leave now,' he says, 'and we will not kill you. We mean no harm to strangers, only to accursed Epidaurus, and its protector Asclepius.'

Do you accept their offer and leave at once (go to **6**)?

Or do you attack them before they can seize your other arm (go to **333**)?

447

You ask for your stake, and the charioteer returns it. 'Good luck in the race,' he says. Go to **169**.

448

The monster is Might 16, Protection 10.

If you attack it, turn to **533**.

If you wait, and hope that the monster is a creature of Poseidon and means you no harm, turn to **371**.

449

You are thanked profusely for your help as a hero, for releasing them from ill-bearing death and fear, and returning their pride and their sacred shrine. As token of their joy, they pile your ship high with provisions and offer you a gift, either an onyx brooch on which is carved the figure of an old man, or a leather pouch which contains a wooden twig. Do you take the brooch (**593**) or the pouch (**95**)?

450

Your pleas for mercy are in vain. The black-cloaked conspirators snatch your sword away from you, and plunge their daggers deep into your stomach. You struggle for a while, but die in terrible agony. If you can pray to Zeus to be saved, you will find yourself at **134**.

451
The rats carried the plague. You have now caught this awful disease from an infected bite. If Asclepius if Neutral to you, go to 377; if you are in Disfavour with him, go to 98.

452
Aeolus, lord of the winds and weather, is not kind to you, and the way to Delos is hard, the ship furrowing the sea like a plough across stony ground when the farmer grows tired and can hardly go on. At last the isle of Delos is in sight, cliffs strangely large and glowing in the dawn sun. The sailors make ready to land, their long-flowing hair blowing in the breeze. At your landing you are greeted by the headman of the island, who implores you to save them, for an evil man has taken up residence at the temple of Apollo and will not move. Perhaps you could drive him away. The man implores you once again, and his robe of green and long white beard seem strangely pathetic.

Do you agree to help and fight the man (465)?

Or do you feel too weakened by the voyage to risk a fight before Crete (296)?

453
When you emerge above the waters, you see to your horror the sea-serpent just a few feet away. It turns its head, iridescent in the sunlight, and sees you. There is no hope: it snaps its jaws, and your red blood is spilt in the wine-dark sea, the realm of Poseidon, where Zeus' aid cannot heal you.

454
Take 2 Shame points as normal, but 4 Honour points for the victory, and turn to 218.

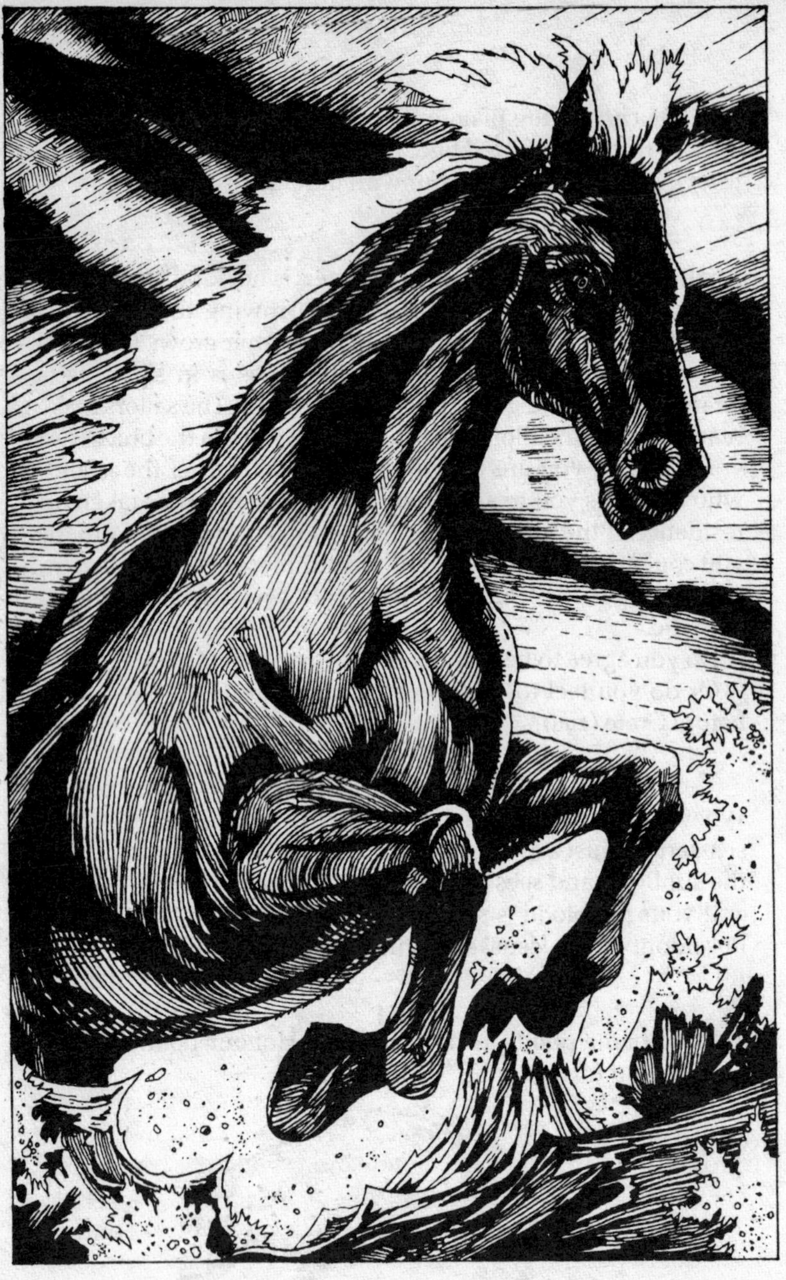

455

You are striding along the beach, deep in thought, remembering your mother's house at Troezen, and your childhood which seems a lifetime ago, but yet is less than a week gone. There is no one else here, perhaps because of the cold sea-breeze driving the birds inland. Out at sea you notice a vessel struggling in the heavy swell. Your musings are suddenly brought to a close by an apparition rising from the sea. A jet-black horse with a golden mane emerges, tosses its head, whinnying, and gallops towards you, hooves printing lightly in the wet sand.

Will you attack the horse (go to 541)?
Will you try to capture it (go to 67)?
Or will you simply avoid it (go to 196)?

456

It is well past dark when you reach Athens, but spiteful Fear has no hold on your heart as you tread the gloom-filled streets. Straight to the palace you go, the guards letting you in with alacrity, wonderment in their eyes. To the feast-hall you go, and all are there assembled, waiting to see if you would return. Seeing you, they cry out in amazement, as the man who has sent a son off to the war, knowing in his heart that he will not return, rejoices and is glad at his return, and yet feels sorrow for what he has done.

So it is that Aegeus greets you, not at first with joy, but with perplexity. Yet his face soon lights up with the brilliant joy that comes from Zeus. He takes the bull's horn, looks at you fondly and says, 'Welcome to my house, Altheus, for you are indeed my son!' Go to 50.

457

You sink to your knees and beg for mercy. The guards sneer at you, and with their companions (for you notice that two more have come upon you from behind, and two stood at the other side of the kitchen), they strip you of all your armour and weapons. With one last look at the silent servants standing with their pots and great bronze cauldrons, evidence of some great feast in preparation, you are dragged off into the palace by your captors. Go to 459.

458

Grim-hearted Hecate herself stands before you; the statue on the altar has disappeared. She stays the assault of the infernal beast.

'Do not think, Altheus,' she says, 'that you have escaped my wrath. The Olympians have stayed my hand this once, but next time you will not be smiled on by Fate.'

The room seems to spin round and round, Hecate disappears and you are engulfed in darkness. Go to **337**.

459

You are pushed down a hallway, feebly protesting and explaining your real identity. 'So it's the king's son you are now, is it?' one of them mocks, as you are shoved into a tiny, dark and bare prison-cell. How, you ask yourself, can a man be prisoner in his own father's household? Surely he should be an honoured guest. Go to **185**.

460

The market-wardens, burly men dressed in blue cloaks and armed with heavy canes, seize you from behind. Before you have time to react, you are being dragged into the centre of the market-square. There, with everyone looking on, you are savagely beaten until you can take no more. Stretched to the limit of your physical endurance, you cry out for mercy, but no mercy comes. At last, when you almost wish that you are dead, the beating ceases. Your back raw and bloody, you are cast out of Megara in disgrace. Take 3 Shame points, and count yourself lucky you are not a citizen; you would have been executed. Go to **86**.

461
Your weariness has befuddled your brains. There is nothing to fear. Lose 1 Honour point, and return to **441**.

462
The two bandits have Might 4, Protection 10, but carry long knives (Might 2, Protection 0). Remember the bonus to the first bandit's Might, because he has one companion (his Might is 7: 4 + 2 + 1).

If they are Seriously Wounded, go to **600**.
If you surrender, go to **374**.
If you die and are saved by Zeus, go to **536**.
If you retreat, go to **536**.

463
Alas! Zeus will not save those whose crime is that they have attacked the Furies, the bringers of divine justice. Your spirit leaves your tortured body, and it is not to the Elysian fields of bliss it will fly, but perhaps to the torments of grim Tartarus.

464

As a feather-shafted arrow by chance hits a man far away in the forest, so your harpoon strikes a spot beneath the water. A creamy yellow liquid flows into the wine-dark sea. Talos groans, and there is a strange squeaking and scratching sound; he sways dangerously, and falls with a crash. You can see his eyes, and within them resides a strange, unearthly intelligence. Talos seems not to be dead. Perhaps only an immortal can kill him. Nevertheless, have 8 Honour points, and turn to 384.

465

You are conducted past the great marble buildings of the tiny isle, to the place where Apollo has his sanctuary, the place of his birth, a gift from Poseidon in exchange for Calauria. Before the temple gates stands a man robed in black, wearing black armour, with a sword of deepest night, as if it were a heavenly blade cast out from the sky, and charred and burnt in its descent to Delos. 'Stranger,' he croaks, his voice hoarse and hard, 'fight or die!'

You must fight. The man has Might 7, Protection 13 (including sword Might 2, greaves Protection 1, breastplate Protection 3). For this fight only, subtract 2 from your Might because of seasickness.

If you surrender, turn to 121.
If you die, and are saved by Zeus, turn to 570.
If you retreat, turn to 387.
If you Seriously Wound your opponent, turn to 519.

466

The climb is hard and takes its toll from your wearied limbs. You pass the outbuildings of the great temple, almost unnoticed in your eagerness to hear the words of the living god.

The white-marbled shrine is awesome indeed; crowds of pilgrims throng before the temple steps, like bees around the honey-pot unaware of the danger that lurks near by. You ascend the steps, pushing through the mob, and enter the temple itself through high-arched gates decorated in huge gems with the deeds of the god. You leave your weapons outside and enter. Turn to **297**.

467

One of the nymphs spots you, and cries out to her companions. A satyr gestures to you, beckoning, and soon you find nymphs pulling you into the dance. You try to resist but it is to no avail. Go to **10**.

468

You pray to your patron Poseidon. Lose 2 Honour points and go to **599**. Alternatively, if you cannot do this, return to **448**.

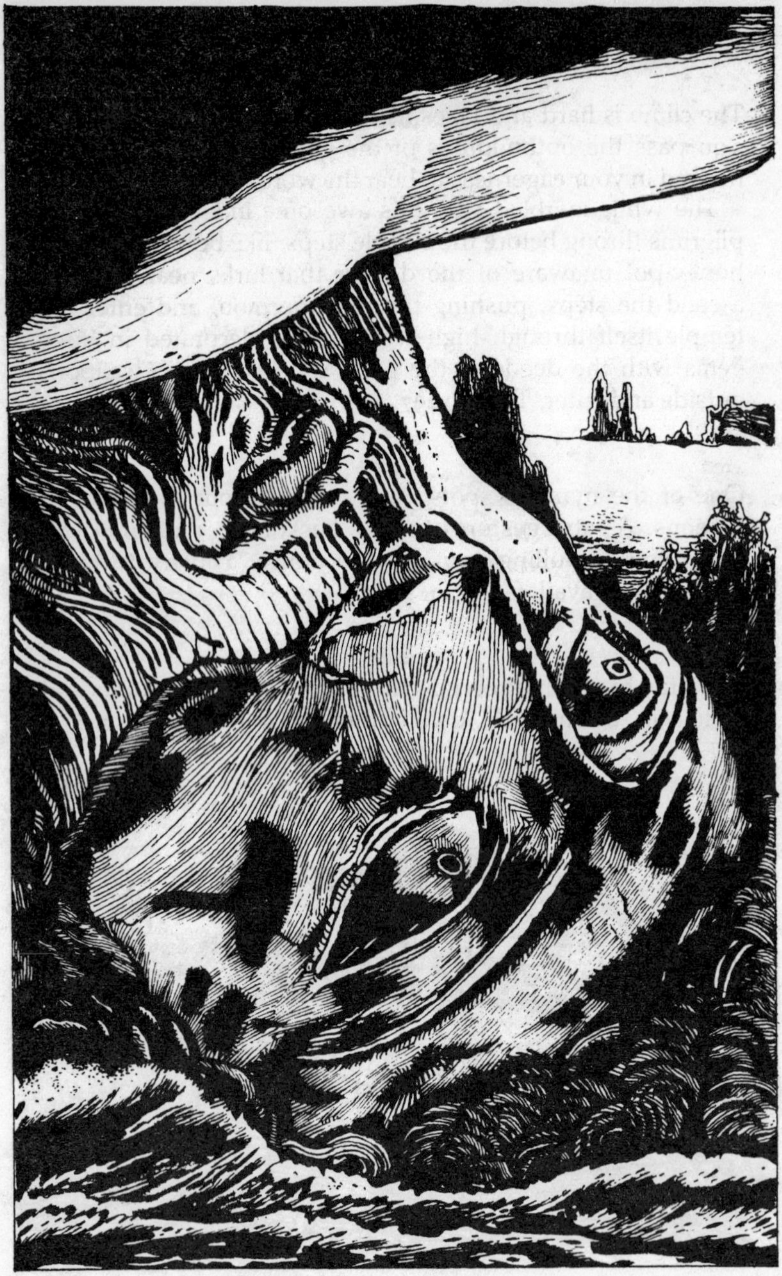

469

The last of the ichor spills and Talos is but an empty vessel. His metallic body sways and crashes, stiff and lifeless. Yet when the ship goes closer to look at this wonder of the Cretan realm, some glimmer of life seems to remain in its deep yellow eyes. It is perhaps true that only by the decree of Olympian Zeus can this being be truly killed. Go to **384**.

470

The market is large, larger than that of Corinth, a fact which surprises you. Perhaps it is something to do with the festival of Hera. There are rumours that the temple has been defiled, and someone must pay with their life. There are merchants here from all parts of Greece – from Arcadia, Achaia, Boeotia, Attica, and even far-off Thessaly and mountainous Epirus. Yet with large gatherings there come less savoury visitors than amicable Altheus. At one stall selling food, you see a group of scruffy men. They seem to be stealing, while one of their number distracts the vendor. Surprised by this, you are forced to make a quick decision.

Do you alert the trader (go to **287**)?

Do you attack the men yourself (go to **63**)?

Do you join in and take full advantage of the opportunity of some free food (go to **219**)?

471

With a shock, you remember what your patron, fair-faced Aphrodite, told you. Grim terror strikes at your heart: perhaps it is too late. You warn the captain to steer to the east. A great shadow seems to blot out the sun, and Talos comes from the west, bellowing his rage, striding ever faster to catch the ship, his bronze body reflecting the sun's rays, like the shining beacon of a funeral pyre. Yet he is too far away. A rock thrown by Talos crashes down some way from the ship. A water spout cascades all over the decks, but you are safe. Talos is too far away to do you any damage, and the ship sails in towards shore and your destination. As you go in, you see that the giant has fallen over. Go to **336**.

472

The drop is dangerous, but with one last glance at the guards pressing into the room behind, you jump, and to your surprise land safely. A javelin clatters on the cobbles beside you, and you run as if the Furies were on your tail. Go to **134**

473

As you hurry on by, the man screams out under the harsh lash of the Furies. 'May you ever regret that you abandoned me,' he cries, 'and may you too be afflicted by these creatures one day.' Have 2 Shame points, and go to **167**.

474

The way to Athens is pleasant. The path is well made, and not rutted like others upon which you have travelled. Soon you pass into an area of green-clad rolling hills, and beyond this the outer edge of Athens' cultivated area. In the distance you can see farmers carrying their allotted portion for distribution to other areas. Your stomach feels light, and you are tense with anticipation.

Suddenly, you can see the very walls of Athens, your goal for so many days. Your pace quickens, and without speaking to anyone you pass, you hurry on, until the great gates of the city are but a few yards away. Go to **40**.

475

The ship is now repaired for the long journey ahead. Everything except the figurehead is replaced, but this cannot be, save on one festival day of the year when the priests of the city's patron may bless it, and instil it with her power. You must traverse the seas without this protection, but if fearsome Poseidon is merciful, then the slender flame of your life's course may burn on to the Cretan shores.

The captain is unsure now which route he should take for Crete. He must go ashore at fire-pent Thera, home of lame Hephaestus, god of fire and craft, but either Melos or Apollo's isle of Delos seem equally balanced for the intervening stop. The gnarled and sea-wise man turns to you for advice.

Do you suggest Melos (**358**), or Delos (**452**)?

476

Sleep and weariness once more take hold of your tired body. At last you open your eyes, and find that your surroundings have changed. You are no longer in your bed-chamber at Aegeus' palace!

If you are in Disfavour with Hecate, go to **585**.

Otherwise, turn to **612**.

477

You are tossed and turned for what seems like days. At last you lose consciousness, and when you wake, you find yourself washed up on a sandy beach, fringed with tall trees. There is no sign of the ship or the serpent. You are stranded here, perhaps for ever. Few other ships will pass by. When you left Athens there was talk of an expedition against high-walled Ilium of the Trojans. Perhaps if it comes soon, you will be found. Otherwise, you must build yourself a vessel; but, alas, heroes have little skill as shipwrights.

478

The road to Delphi is long and hard, and you soon realize that you will not make it in a single day. Late in the afternoon of the fifth you see ahead a small band of travellers and you hurry towards them trying to catch up. By their plain garb, you can see that they are pilgrims, most probably making, as you are, for the archer god's sanctuary at Delphi. You see that they are carrying gifts of jewellery, gold and silver for the god. You realize that you have no comparable gift.

Do you try to force the pilgrims to give you something by attacking them (turn to **260**)?

Do you join them and try to buy something from them (turn to **483**)?

Or do you press on regardless, trusting in your heroic prowess to impress the god (turn to **57**)?

479

You unbuckle the shining armour and hand it to the wretch. He licks his juice-covered fingers before taking it, but still stains it by his touch. 'No need of this,' he cries. 'The best defence is to approach Crete before noon.' He turns and flees, trailing his filthy rags behind him. You cry out to him, but it is no use. You pick up the discarded armour, and walk back to the ship. Have 1 Honour point, and go to **583**.

480

The priest takes your money with a look of gleeful disdain on his face. He leads you out of the temple and on to the forecourt. Go to **115**.

481

The charioteer shrugs nonchalantly. 'This will do. Your wager is on the green chariot.' Go to **391**.

482

The queen blanches and tries to push the goblet away. 'The wine is poisoned!' you cry. There is a great commotion, and in the confusion Medea escapes from the feasting-hall. From her dress, as she flees, falls the pouch of white powder. An Athenian noble picks it up, sniffs it and says, 'The stranger was right; this is poison.' The king turns to you, the hero whom his wife sought to kill. Turn to **170**.

483

The pilgrims are friendly, and are indeed on their way to Delphi to worship at the archer god's shrine. They tell you something of the road ahead. You must pass through Cirrha, but this is within the sacred plain of Delphi, where nothing should be cultivated. You admire one of the effigies of the god, and a fair-haired woman offers it to you, but you insist that she takes some money for it. She accepts and you carry on down the road. The sky darkens, and it seems there might be a storm. The other pilgrims stop at a roadside hostel which caters for travellers on their way to Delphi; but you press onwards to Cirrha, anxious to get as far as you may before nightfall. Go to 339.

484

The beast comes back towards the black ship, and the clash as you meet is mighty. The sun's rays on your armour are as sparks from a fire, and the din of your encounter makes it seem as if the very sky is not secure in its place.

If you die and are saved by Zeus, turn to 29.

If you Seriously Wound the serpent, turn to 582.

If you retreat, turn to 523.

485

Ah Altheus, there is no aid before such a battle to save the very sanctuary of Apollo! Lose 1 Honour point, and return to 465.

486

Many have thought of stealing the god's jewels. None have succeeded. Have 1 Shame point, and go to 297.

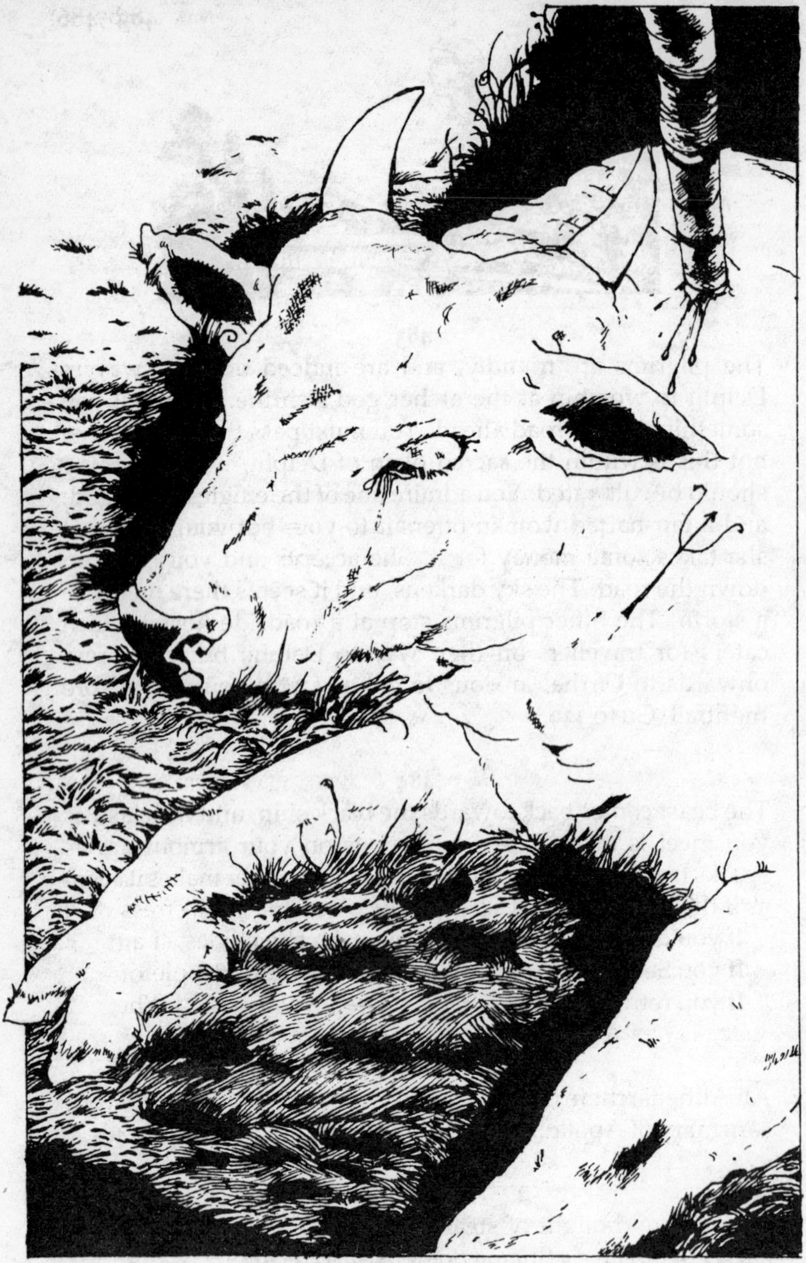

487

A great cheer comes from the assembled company, as from those who know they have overcome their opponents in the swift encounter, and their spirits are haughty. Yet joy departs, and horror seizes all when they examine the cow. Upon its neck is the mark of a trident. This is one of the cattle of Poseidon's herd you have killed. You hurry back to the ship, each man fearful of the vengeance of the god.

If Poseidon is your patron, he will not aid you until you have sacrificed 6 Honour points. Otherwise, take 4 Shame points, and you are in Disfavour with Poseidon. Go to **323**.

488

You may either spend 1–3 Honour points for Ares' aid (roll one die: 1–2 = 1 point, 3–4 = 2 points, 5–6 = 3 points) and turn to **307**, or lose 1 Honour point and go to **136**.

489

You approach the crowd. 'Friends,' you say, 'is this what we expect of the folk of Athens, proud and free, but gentle too? Why do you stone these foreigners? What harm have they done you?'

If you have 13 or more points of Shame, go to **214**.

If you have less than 13 Shame points, go to **502**.

490

As you seek to leave the place, the divine protectress of the town herself bars the way. 'Altheus,' she chides, 'I am most displeased with you for failing to aid these people of mine. Your twip to Cwete will now be vewy wough. When you appwoach Athens, expect no help fwom me at your awwival.' If your patron is Athena then go to **156**; otherwise the goddess disappears, and you may go on your way, with 1 Shame point, and the Disfavour of Athena. Go to **51**.

491

If you accept the aid of the white-armed queen Aphrodite, spend 2–4 Honour points (roll 1 die, divide by 2, round up, and then add 1), and turn to **590**. If you do not, lose 1 Honour point, and turn to **54**.

492

Away from blessed Delos the ship flies across the water towards Hephaestus' isle of Thera. Your weary limbs feel better now, and you are able to walk on the deck, admiring the waters and the craggy isles you pass, except when squalls suddenly come and send you scurrying beneath, feeling as if your body is riddled with feathered arrows.

At last the ship comes in sight of Thera, where the Phoenicians dwell. Go to **295**.

493

You run away, caught up in the general panic. This is no action fitting of a hero, to flee the chance to deliver the town from its scourge. Have 1 extra Shame point, and go to **378**.

494

As you reach the spot where the procession stands, you notice, with a start, that it is no bundle of sticks these people carry, but the corpse of a man dressed in coarse woollen garments, dyed red with the blood that has poured from a gash in his stomach. One young woman notices you and screams, pointing at you. 'This is the man,' she cries. 'He must be a retainer of the king. See his fine robes. Let us kill him!' The mob charges you, and you must defend yourself.

These unskilled fighters act as a group, with one attack only: Might 8, Protection 11. Each time you score a hit, one of the men is killed, and the Might score is reduced by one.

If you retreat, turn to **407**.
If you die, and are saved by Zeus, you find yourself at **230**.
If you surrender, turn to **556**.
When you have killed five men, turn to **151**.

495
The mighty-masted ship is now prepared for the long sail from Thera to Crete. The captain pours a libation of red wine into the waters, praying to great Poseidon for safe passage. The wind, which starts strong, so that the ship can sail under its doom-black sails, bearing its blood-cargo to Crete, soon builds up to a storm.

If Poseidon is your patron, but will not aid you, or you are in Disfavour with Poseidon, go to **568**.

If Poseidon is Neutral towards you, go to **125**.

If Poseidon is your patron and will aid you, or you are in Favour with Poseidon, go to **342**.

496
Dreams played an important part in Greek legend and society, and were often said to be sent by the gods. Take 1 Shame point and lose 1 Honour point. Return to **476**.

497
You stay alert for some hours, but there is no sound, save for the screeching of the owl as it breaks the back of its tiny prey. At length you succumb to soft-tongued Sleep's gentle persuasion. Go to **411**.

498

The beast moans in its agony, with malice in its tone, and thrashes; deep red gore gushes from its gaping wound. It turns to retreat, but as it goes the blood attracts its brothers and it is ripped to pieces in an unholy feast. Fearful lest the serpents turn on his vessel the captain orders the ship under way, pausing only long enough to allow you to scramble aboard. Have 7 Honour points for your feat, and go to **349**.

499

Have 1 Shame point, but go to **309**.

500

You awake to find that Procrustes the innkeeper has chopped off both of your legs to make you fit the bed. As you bleed to death, you have just enough time to gasp a prayer to Zeus to save you. If you have not called on him yet in this adventure, turn to **118**. Otherwise, the travels of Altheus end here . . .

501

The man is still where the Furies left him, almost unable to move from fear. You shake him, and show him that all is well. He thanks you profusely, relief clear on his face.

'I killed my wife,' he confesses. 'It was an accident, but the Furies won't listen. Perhaps now I have time to gain sanctuary in the temple of Athena. Whatever happens, I will have no use for this.' He takes from around his bloodied neck a gold chain on which hangs an amulet of red rubies. 'Here, this will aid you in fights with mortal creatures.'

While wearing the ruby amulet, your Might value is increased by 2 *or* your Protection is increased by 2. The choice is yours, but you cannot switch the advantage to the other attribute in the middle of a combat. Note also that to invoke it, you must forgo your first attack to pray to your patron. If you are defeated in combat and you lose a weapon, this will count as a combined Might/Protection value of 5, and not 4.

Thanking you once again, the man stumbles off towards Athens and possible safety. Go to **167**.

502

If you have more than 14 Honour points, go to **62**. If you have less than 15 Honour points, go to **312**.

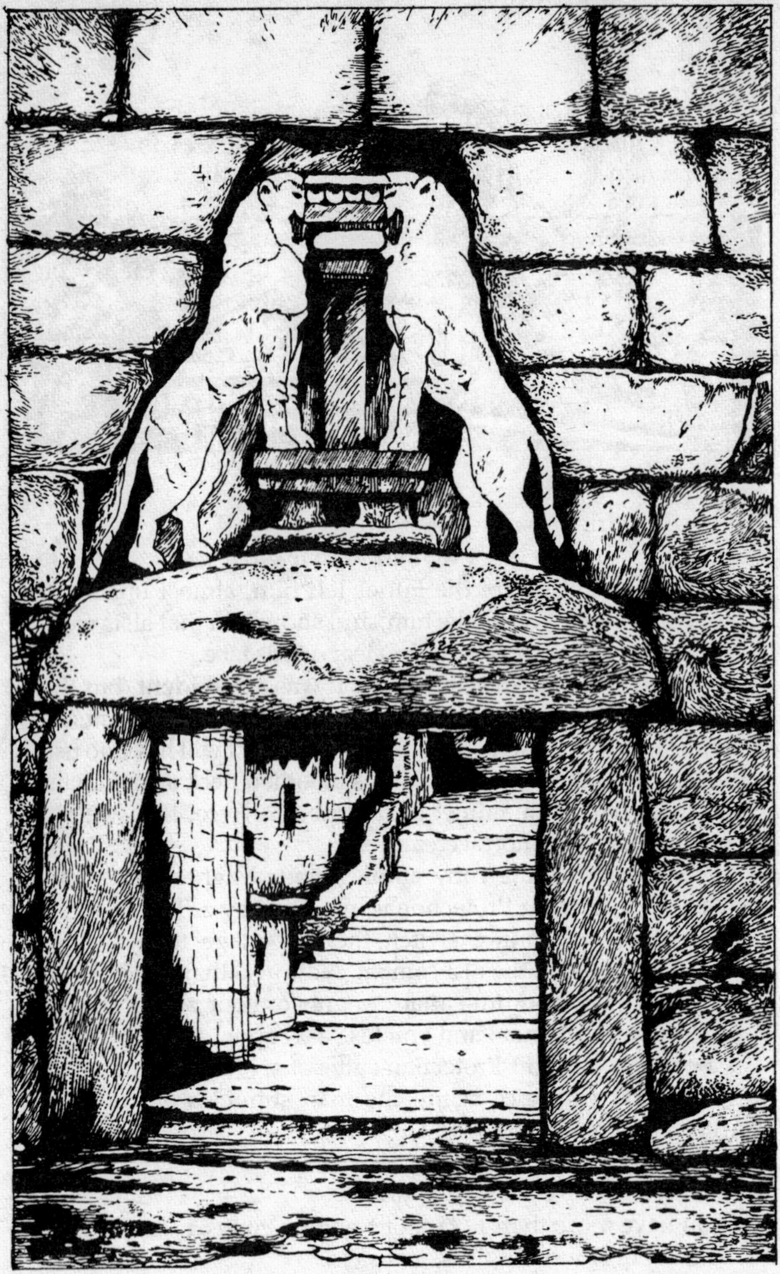

503

You come to Mycenae, and are awestruck by the magnificence of the lion gate. Can this, you think to yourself, be the work of earth-bound mortals? No, truly, these are the works of the one-eyed Cyclopes, giant offspring of Earth's son, Uranus. You carry on into the city itself; on the summit of the heaven-pointing mount, the palace of the king towers up above the city. The people carry on their business, almost unaware of the fort above where the soldiers look out, in case any enemy should try to come upon the city unawares, as a hungry wolf creeps up upon the sheep-pen, with the shepherd asleep, his head dulled by wine. Past the market-place you walk, and at length you come to a stream. Many women are beating their clothes dry on the stones beside the bank.

Do you drink some of the water (go to **193**)?

Or do you carry on through Mycenae (go to **12**)?

504

When awareness returns to your sea-battered brain, the serpent has gone. Three of the oarsmen have been rent and torn asunder by its jaws, like houses that are blown away by the wind that gusts suddenly and is gone, leaving the folk of the place to bewail their fate and cry for their sons and daughters who were so young.

The captain gathers together the remaining crew and you get under way as fast as possible, before the sea-snake can return. Go to **349**.

505

Feeling in the pocket of your tunic, you find the gem your mother gave to you when you left Troezen. You hold it out to King Aegeus, who looks at it astonished. 'I am Altheus,' you say, 'and this is the proof.'

Aegeus' regal posture relaxes and he smiles. 'I welcome you, my son, come at last and unawaited to the palace of your father!' Go to **50**.

506

With the words of the conspirators still ringing in your ears, you get up and leave the inn, trying not to look too conspicuous. You ask a passer-by the quickest way to the palace, but she looks at you strangely, and simply points towards the centre of the town. The palace, in fact, is not difficult to find. The door is bound with metal strips, and it is a while before a guard emerges to answer your knocking. You tell of what you have heard in the inn, and he demands that you relinquish all your weapons, and place them on a table beside the doorway.

He leads through the great hall, hung with tapestries, to the main throne-room where the king is entertaining some guests. The assembly falls silent, and the king demands to know who disturbs his feast.

You explain what you have heard, but the king laughs and does not believe you. He orders you to be seized and locked in the storeroom for the night, and to be whipped the following morning.

'No one,' he booms, 'would plot against *me*!' Go to **17**.

507

You take the shield (Might 0, Protection 2) and spear (Might 2, Protection 0), and leave the camp of the warrior women. The Amazon, being an honourable opponent, does not raise the alarm. Have 5 Honour points for your victory, and go to **320**.

508

You are travelling along a road, deeply rutted by the carts of pilgrims bringing sick ones or gifts to the temple of the healer. Beside the road the trees and bushes rustle menacingly. The wind whips up spirals of dust from the track, which further obscure the way ahead. Go to **20**.

509

You stride into the swirling stream, leaving the woman behind. The going is hard, as the stream is deeper than you had thought. Behind you, you can hear the hag screaming something. You listen briefly. If Hera is your patron, go to **46**. If not, go to **261**.

510

Through the mass of corpses you wade, like one traversing a river of blood and gore, pushing aside the dogs and ravens, which have already begun to claim their spoils of war. It is clear to you that the Athenians are the victors and hold the field. With joy in your heart you make your way to Aegeus' palace. Go to **283**.

511

As the morning mists clear you see Delphi for the first time. Behind it Mount Parnassus rises, its snow-capped peak rising almost to heaven, its slopes thickly wooded, the haunt of dryads and their nymphly kin. All around to the north the rocky mountains imprison the temple in its deep-set valley, cleft in the centre by two great cliffs. From this issues the Castalian spring, its clear waters flowing down the slopes, past the Nauplian rock, from which forbidding crag by custom criminals are cast. You go on up the slope to Delphi. Go to **466**.

512

Almighty Zeus, guardian of the heavens, speaks to you directly from his Olympian throne. 'I cannot help you greatly, Altheus, for to do so would overturn the decree of another god, and this I may not do while time runs its allotted span. Yet I can infuse your limbs again with the life that is leaving them. Go now and face the curse of Hecate.'

You must face the black dog once more, restored to an Unwounded state, but with only 1 Honour point. Go to **585**.

513

You lie awake all night, occasionally hearing the clattering of wheels on the cobbles and the shouts of the spectators. You wish that you had gone to see them, and not remained in bed like a feeble old warrior. In the morning you eat a meagre breakfast and trudge off dejectedly towards Athens. Go to **474**.

514

The nobleman shrugs his shoulders, and confesses that he too is a stranger in Athens, hailing from far-off Pylos. Without another word he rushes off into the crowd, afraid lest he be singled out as a foreigner.

You must now go either to the left (**90**) or the right (**580**).

515

You turn to flee, but there, barring your way, stands Olympian Zeus, radiant in his glory. The light and splendour of his presence overcome you and burn out your eyes. Writhing in agony, you plead to be forgiven for forsaking your destiny. 'This favour only shall I grant you, snivelling cur,' thunders Zeus, his voice reverberating through the valleys as the crash of a mighty wave: 'release.' With this the feeble candle of your life is snuffed out by a lightning bolt, and your spirit passes into the dark realms of Hades.

516

A look of horror descends on the face of the Amazon as she realizes that you are going to kill her. 'May the curse of Hera be upon you for killing Hippia,' she cries out, and with this a mist of darkness clouds her eyes, and she is dead. You take her shield (Might 0, Protection 2) and spear (Might 2, Protection 0). You may have 5 Honour points for your victory, but must take 2 Shame points as usual for killing an opponent who has surrendered. You are also in Disfavour with Hera, if she is not your patron. Go to 320.

517

The Amazon is Might 7, Protection 14, including a spear (Might 2) and lionskin (Protection 2). Because she has surprised you, she will have the first thrust in combat.

If you Seriously Wound the Amazon, turn to 159.

If you surrender, turn to 550.

If you retreat, turn to 165.

If you die, and are saved by Zeus, you find yourself at 165.

If, when it is your turn to strike, you try to explain that you are not in the camp as an intruder, but as a peace-maker, turn to 606.

518

As the men run off down the streets and disappear, you realize that you cannot simply keep what you have heard to yourself. You set off towards the centre of the town, where the great white palace of the Theban kings stands, a memorial to more glorious times. Go to 313.

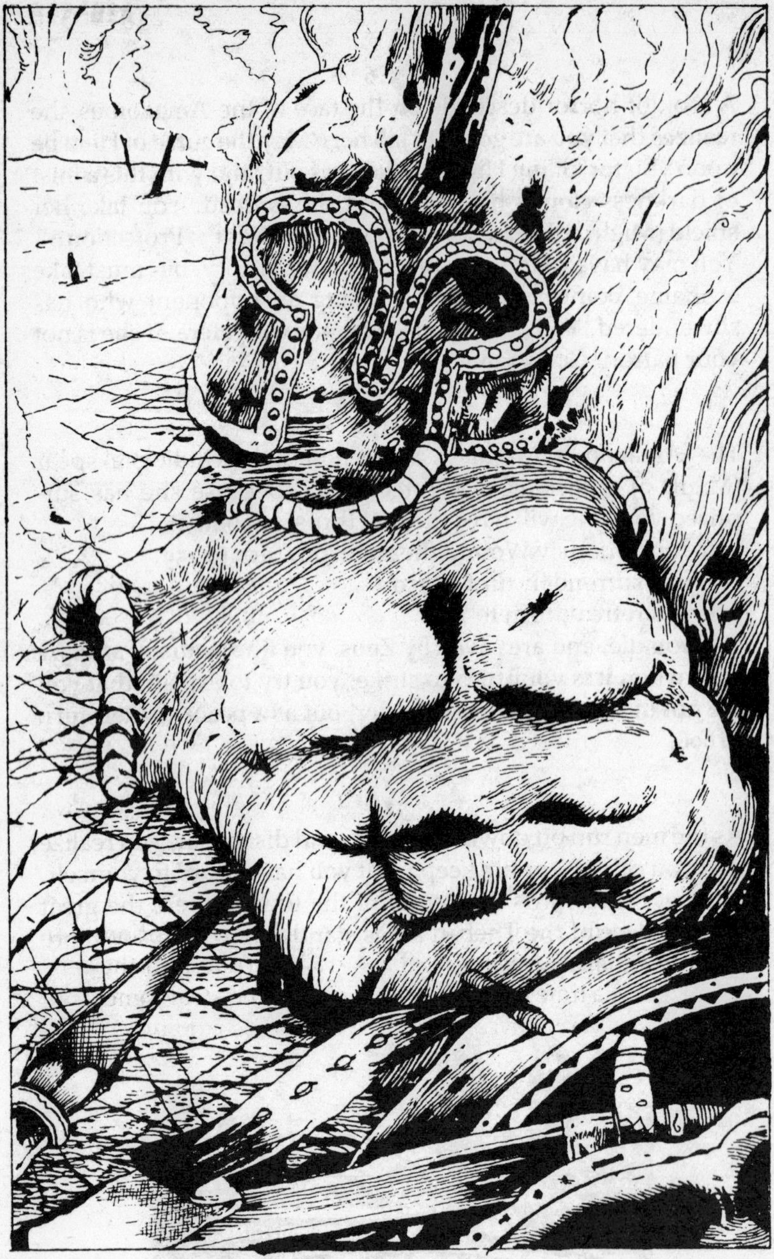

519

As your blade strikes through the body of the man, his visage seems to dissolve and his body to crumple and vanish. All that is left is a heap of charred armour and weapons, burning their imprint into the ground, as the fire that ravages the god-favoured citadel. Have 5 Honour points for your victory, and go to **254**.

520

Lose 1 extra Honour point for abandoning the man to his fate. As you approach the water's edge, you can hear his screams and pleas to the Olympians, unanswered as those of the rich man set upon by thieves, whom his neighbours will not help, for fear of being killed themselves. Go to **167**.

521

Expecting to see the Pythian priestess, you are stunned to see your patron god Apollo seated at a table, apparently working; manuscripts are strewn all around the floor, and ink-marks stain one arm of his tunic. 'I was just working on some prophecies,' he says. 'This one's for Naxos and it's a few centuries overdue. I'm afraid you can't have one now, but do come and see me at Delos.' With this the god dismisses you and you leave quickly. Collect your weapons, and go on down towards Thebes (**191**).

522

Have 1 Shame point for agreeing to such a proposition. You leave the market quickly as the wardens try to find the thief again. After a time he suggests you return and steal some food. You are so deeply involved that you agree. Go to **219**.

523

Where can you retreat to, Altheus? Below decks? Into the wine-dark sea? Take 1 additional Shame point, and return to **484**.

524

The unnatural storm has subsided, but soon the still, glassy waters ripple under the breath of another gale. The crewmen are hard put to keep the high-prowed vessel afloat, and the Athenians cower in a corner, praying for a few days more to add to their wretched lot. Poseidon has not been kind. Go to **363**.

525

Cythnos is not a busy isle. Few ships from Athens stop here, and you are soon waylaid by a bent old man, asking for tales from Athena's city. You oblige, telling of the exploits of your brother Theseus, sadness in your heart for the loss you have suffered. When you have finished, it is late. Tired and hungry – for in your eagerness you have forgotten to eat – you return to the harbour. Go to **279**.

526

You may have 4 Honour points for killing the bear. Tired out by the exertion of the fight, you rest for the night by the still-warm corpse of your erstwhile adversary. In the morning you wash in a nearby stream, and make your way quickly back to the road. Go to **13**.

527

You may have 3 Honour points for your victory. If you want to, and are able, you may take and use her shield (Protection 2) and spear (Might 2). Turn to **102**, and choose another opponent.

528

As the path narrows, the rustling of the trees seems less natural. You dive into the undergrowth and, as you creep stealthily, you find that your fears are well founded, for two swarthy-looking men armed with long knives lie in wait for unwary passers-by.

Do you challenge them to fight (go to **462**), or do you simply attack them without warning (go to **221**)?

529

To confirm her supplication the Amazon queen gives you the jewelled brooch from her shoulder. 'If you see Lembra, this will tell her that you are my friend,' she says. Go to **385**.

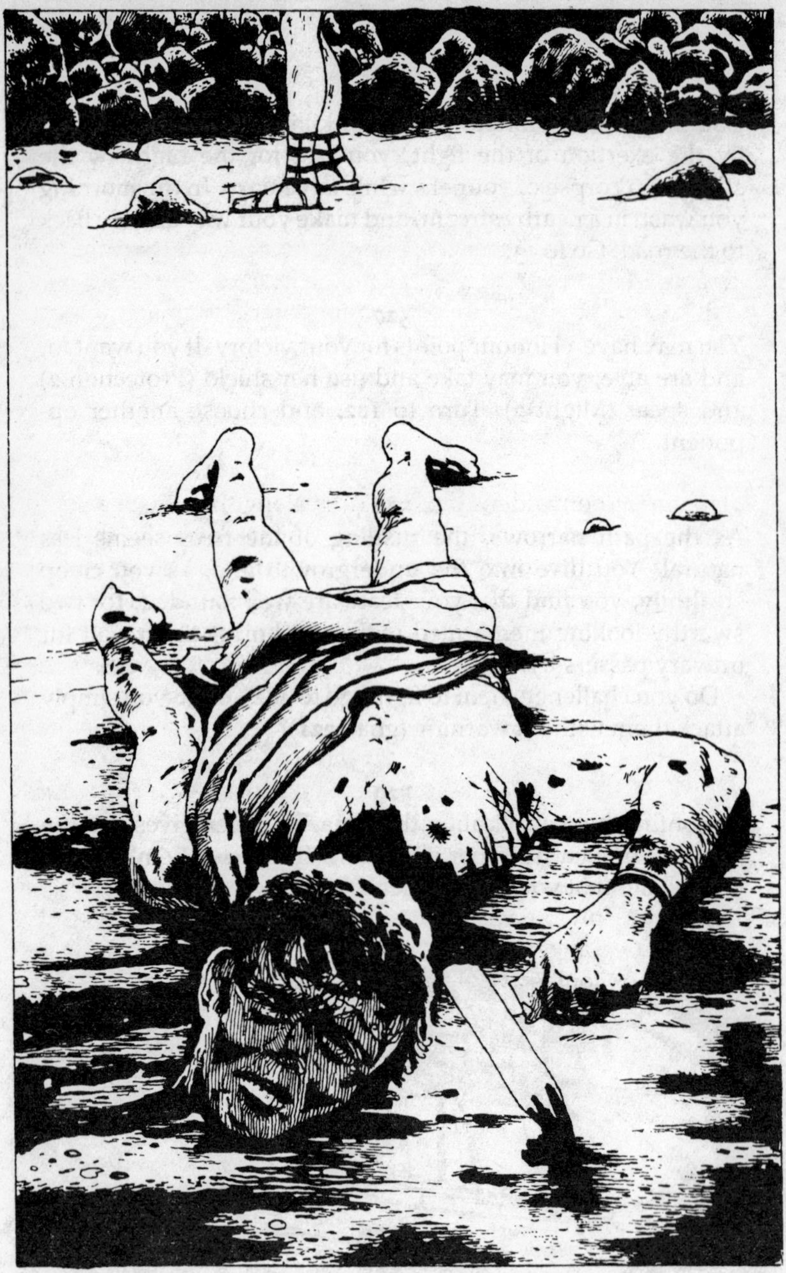

530

Feeling in your scabbard you realize that by accident you have taken the captain's sword (Might 2). No matter: this wretch will not put up a fight. You lop his head from his shoulders. For a second there is an expression of astonishment on his face, and then it is covered with the blood that spurts from the stump. Both head and body fall to the ground, and the tongue lolls on to the sand. Have 5 Shame points for this gruesome deed.

You return closer to the ship, in case anyone should see what you have done. Go to 583.

531

The track soon widens out and runs along the side of a small stream. You stop and quench your thirst. Ahead in the distance you sight a town, and press on towards it. You are almost there when a man mounted on a horse gallops down the road towards you. As he approaches, you shout to him, asking what city this might be. He has time only to utter one word before he passes beyond you: 'Acharnae!' Go to 116.

532

You rush through the falling stones and rocks, to try to rescue the fair-faced lady, but when you reach the spot, she has gone, and her gold throne is but another massive boulder. The rock-fall, too, has gone. All the buffeting and danger were for nothing. Only the cripple remains, and the cast of his face is that of deep anger.

'So you would save Hera, who crippled me. So let it be. My curse is on you, and ever may you regret that you abandoned resourceful Hephaestus in the hope of winning glory.'

With this the god is gone, and you stand alone, save for the crewmen, your heroic venture once again turned to ruin. You are in Disfavour with Hephaestus. Go to 495.

533

You realize that you are unarmed: your weapons are still down below. There is little time to decide. You could grab a harpoon, and attack with this (Might 3, Protection 0): go to **318**. Or you could dash down and collect your arms from the hold of the ship (go to **298**).

534

Rushing back to where the old man sat, you find that he was just leaving for whatever miserable hovel he subsists in. You ask him the way to Aegeus' palace. He seems reluctant at first but then says that he has business near by, and it would be no trouble for him to show you the way. Go to **77**.

535

Roll one die. If it is 5 or 6, you hit and kill the cow with your mighty throw (go to **487**). Otherwise, take 1 Shame point, and you may either give in and go back to the ship (go to **323**), or try to wrestle the cow down (go to **565**). If you wish, you can throw another spear instead (remain at **535**).

536

The sun, saffron-robed, has climbed high above you to your left, and now begins her long descent, as you come to the River Cleonae, its waters reflecting her life-giving rays. In the distance you see Cleonae itself, and woods wreathe the banks and the way to the town.

The deep-whirling river is spring-swollen with the melting snow from the mountains, and a shallow ford is the only crossing. An aged crone stands despairing, unable to cross, staring at the muddy waters. 'Pity me,' she pleads, 'for I am old and weak. If you would carry me, I could cross the river. Otherwise I must stay here and stony-hearted Hunger will take me, and it will be you who has killed me.'

Do you attack the woman, and beat stony-hearted Hunger to it (go to **444**)?

Do you throw her in the river and tell her to swim (go to **76**)?

You could cross the river without her (go to **509**).

Or you could carry her across the river (go to **316**).

537
Achilles will be baptized in the Styx, but never would a hero allow himself to be baptized in the blood of a temple defiled by godless men. As your life's spirit leaves you, stained red with your shame, you cry out to Zeus. The god does not listen to your tortured pleas. He will not aid such an unheroic mortal. The adventures of Altheus end here.

538
Owl-faced Athena appears and bars your way to the palace. 'Foolish youth,' she says, 'you have spared these men to warn their companions. You are in tewwible pewil. You cannot wescue the woyal king of Thebes now; you must wush fwom the city. Wun!' With this Athena transforms herself into an owl, and flies to Olympus, keeping upwind of Thebes. Go to 134.

539
You have been wandering around for an hour or more now. Megara is much like any other town, except that the citizens are subdued, and there is little of the pace that you have come to expect from life in large towns. At length you come to a road, wider than any of the others, lined on either side by temples to the various major gods. At the steps of one a small crowd of white-robed citizens stand; it is the temple of Hera. You approach the place, and soon realize that there is some form of ceremony being performed, but it is not until you have almost

reached the temple itself that you see that is no normal temple rite. They are going to sacrifice someone to the goddess! A girl dressed in blue is being dragged down the temple steps towards an altar set up for the purpose and draped in a cloth of deep red. She screams, and calls out for help, but no one moves.

Do you rush up and attempt to save her (go to **398**)?

Or do you just walk away from the place, choosing not to interfere in the ritual (go to **148**)?

540

Each round, starting from the next one, before your attack, Talos loses 3 from each of his attributes, as the yellow ichor leaks into the water and his life-force ebbs. Return to **48**. (Should his values fall to 0 or below, however, turn to **469**.)

541

As your first blow strikes home, the horse rears up as if in pain. Now, sitting on its night-dark back, there is a fearsome rider, Poseidon the horse-tamer, lord of the sea. 'Foolish action,' he says, 'but only to be expected from such a callow youth. Your father would never strike a sacred horse, and nor would your brother. This is just too much. Expect no clement weather on your sea voyages.' With this both horse and rider gallop away under the waves. You must lose 3 Honour points for your dreadful deed, and if Poseidon is your patron, you must also have 1 Shame point. If he is not your patron, you are in Disfavour with him. You carry on down the beach, past Cenchraea and on to Crommyon. After some hours you reach the town itself. Go to **100**.

542
The two men explain, when you approach them, that they were talking of an expedition against the king of high-walled Troy. They offer you a drink, and you take it, still suspicious of them, but wanting to learn more. Within minutes you are feeling drowsy, and you slump to the table unconscious, and oblivious of the great events taking shape around you. Go to 70.

543
Do you try to save the gold-throned woman (532), the lame blacksmith (390), or the mighty warrior (143)?

544
The Amazon has Might 7 (basic 5 + 2 for her spear), Protection 14 (basic 10 + 2 for her hide shield + 2 for the bearskin).

If you pray to your patron for aid before the combat, go to 242.

If you retreat, go to 320.

If you die, and are saved by Zeus, you will find yourself at paragraph 320.

If you surrender, go to 431.

If you Seriously Wound the Amazon, go to 273.

545
You dash in like a death-bringing waterspout from Poseidon's realm, but you are just as forcefully ejected, like a rag doll in a storm. This was the house of the ruler of Cythnos. You lie half unconscious on the muddy floor for an hour. Perhaps it would be better if you returned empty-handed to the ship. Have 1 Shame point, and go to 475.

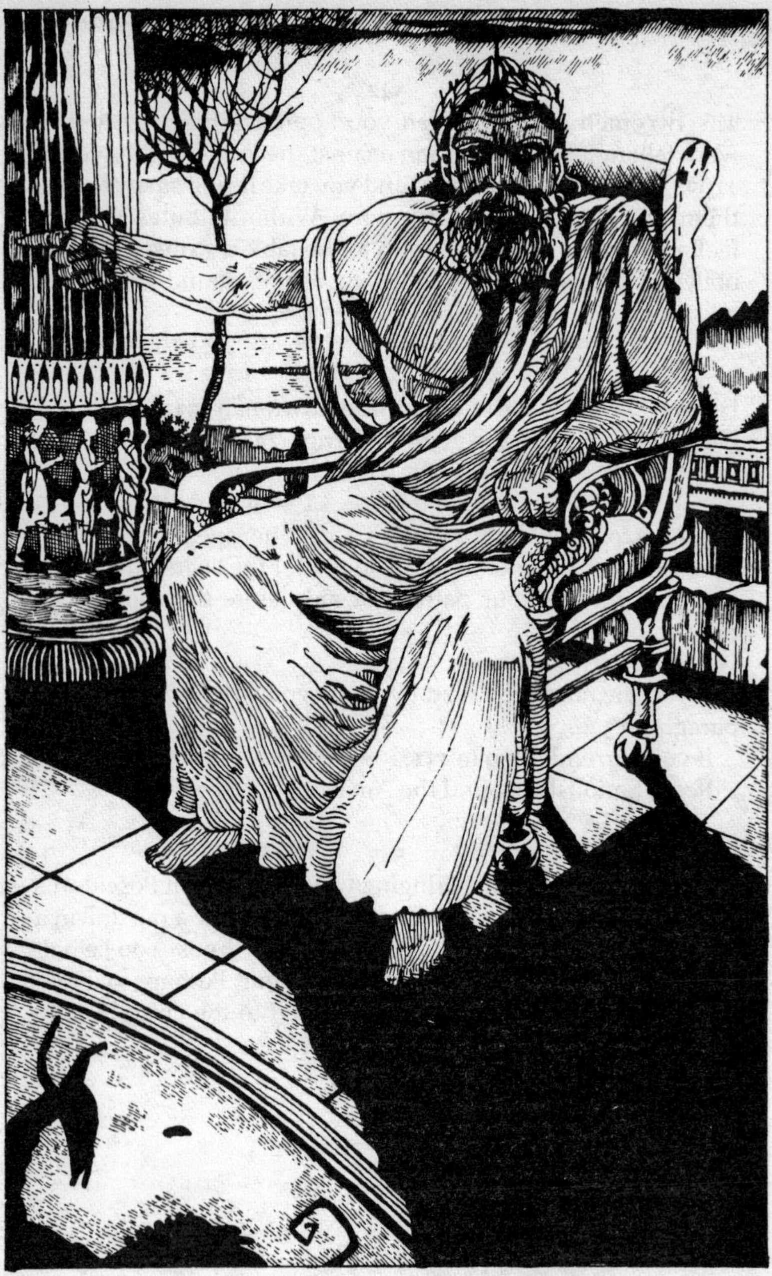

546

For a moment Aegeus is taken aback, but then he continues, 'So you claim to be my high-hearted son amicable Altheus. Yet I have not seen you for many years, and you have shown me no token of kinship. Now there is only one way that you can prove to me that you are Aegeus' younger son, and Theseus' lesser brother.'

The king smiles enigmatically, and then continues, 'There is a bull that strikes terror into the folk around the town of Marathon. Go now and kill this creature; for if you can, then you are truly my son.'

Hearing his words, you do not speak, but stride proudly out of the hall, and, collecting your belongings, set out for Marathon, eager to prove that you are indeed Altheus. Go to **96**.

547

The beast has Might 18, Protection 11. If you attack this spawn of Ocean turn to **533**.

If you say nothing, keeping quiet in case the monstrous serpent has not seen the ship, turn to **562**.

If you call on the god of the sea to help you, turn to **34**.

548

If you have a small silver ear-ring, turn to **108**. Otherwise, take 1 to 6 Shame points (roll a die), and go to **102**.

549

The crashing rocks and the splintering of the ship's wood are too much for you and you order the captain to move the ship away from shore. Slowly he steers it, but then dark fear freezes all your limbs, for Talos follows. Swift as the coming of the storm he treads, breaking and crushing all in his path. Now you must fight the giant at close quarters, his smooth bronze-muscled limbs all the more terrifying.

He is Might (*)14, Protection 18 (regardless of whether you have wounded him earlier or not, he is now Unwounded). There is no hope of retreat.

If you surrender, turn to **443**.
If you kill Talos, turn to **617**.
If you die, turn to **174**.

550

Have 1 Shame point for surrendering. The Amazon stoops to remove your armour so that she may parade it in the camp as token of her victory, and an omen for the next day's battle. She notices the sacred hairpin on your belt, and realizes she has attacked an ambassador. 'Why did you not explain who you were?' she asks. Chastened and shamed, you are led to the queen's tent, without time to bathe your aching wounds. Turn to **8**.

551

Have 1 Shame point for disbelieving the man. Return to **531**.

552

As you turn to leave, you seem to hear a voice, as soft as a nymph's cry, nearly lost in the rustle of the trees under autumn's soothing sun. 'Altheus,' it says, 'thank you. Before I forget, here's a piece of advice:

> *"The flames of Troezen are as nothing to the flames here;*
> *The one with three legs – aid him there."'*

Wondering at these words, surely those of the god, you make your way with powerful strides back to the ship. Go to **449**.

553

Zeus saves you, but warns you that to merit your rebirth, you must go and save the temple of Asclepius. The bandits have long gone, and you travel quickly towards the temple. Go to **508**.

554

The priest takes the golden figure and gazes at it as if entranced. He looks up with a start and leads you to a spot in front of the sanctuary. He tells you to wait for a while, and then he will interpret the Pythian priestess's moan. If you were in Disfavour with Apollo he is now Neutral to you. Go to **181**.

555

Shame on you! The farmer turns round and notices you pilfering his cheese. He shouts at you, grabs you and throws you off the cart on to the ground, where the mule kicks you. Before you can react he has driven away. Have 1 Shame point, and you must walk the rest of the way to Crommyon. At last you reach the town. Go to **100**.

556

You drop to your knees and plead for mercy, trying to explain that you have done nothing. The woman who set off the attack does not relent and directs your assailants to kill you. Your last sight before grim Hades claims your soul is of a sharp scythe glinting in the sunlight and crashing down to your neck – unless, of course, you can pray to Zeus. If so, go to **230**.

557

You crawl into the bottom of the boat wet and bedraggled. 'I was wise to choose you, Altheus, you're so heroic,' whispers the woman sweetly, and you realize that this is none other than your patron, honey-tongued Aphrodite. With a toss of her golden hair she transports you to her Cytherean home. Go to **235**.

558
You hear a blood-curdling scream, like that of a woman, and before your eyes the scene begins to shift and change, like the sands on the sea-shore before the turning of the tide. For defeating the hound of Hecate, you gain no Honour points, because of the curse of the goddess. Go to **337**.

559
You would be well advised to think carefully before making your decision. To save the girl would clearly anger Hera, who would do her best to hinder your quest. On the other hand, to leave the maiden to her fate would undoubtedly displease Aphrodite, goddess of beauty. Go back to **539** and make your choice.

560
You wake with a start, and a headache. You find yourself out in the street, no doubt thrown out by the sullen innkeeper. Your mind recalls the events of the preceding night. You wonder at the ways of conspirators. Have 2 Shame points for trying to join them. Go to **134**.

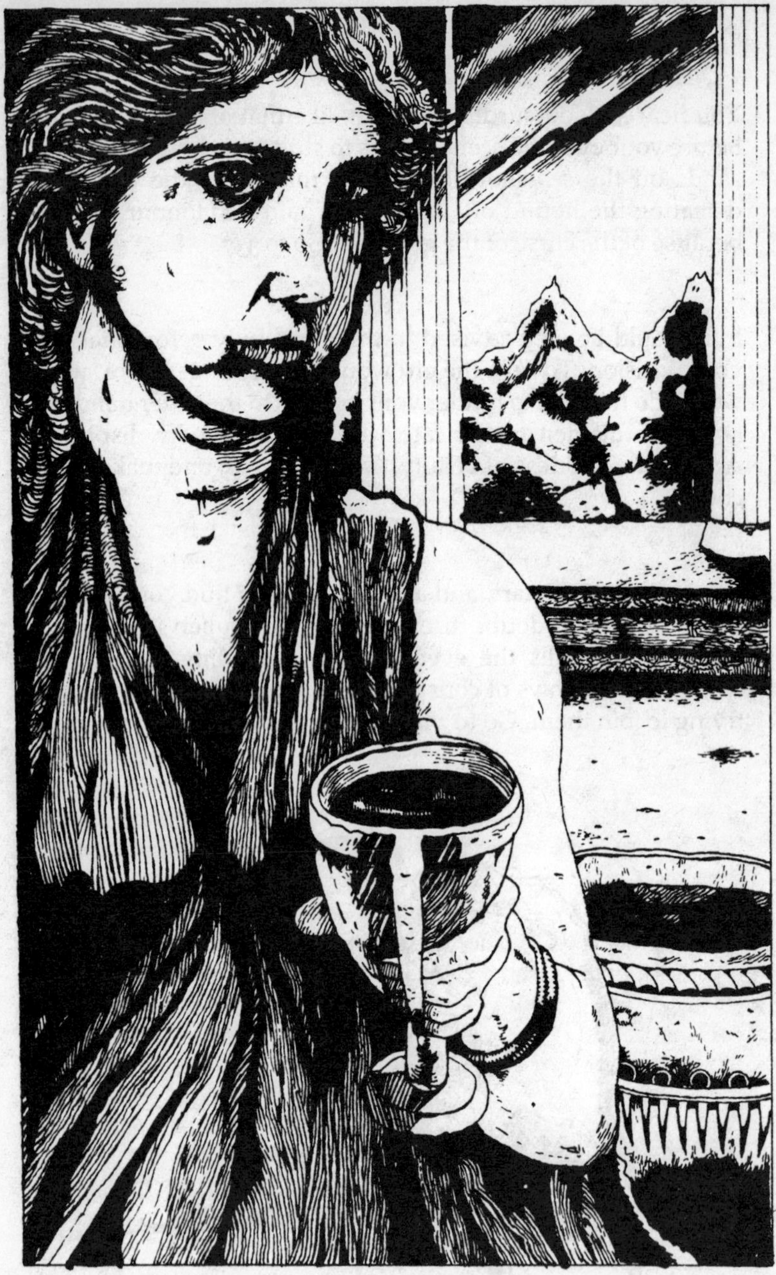

561

Queen Medea, your father's new wife, notices that your goblet is empty. 'Stranger,' she says, 'let me fill your cup.' With this she stands, a woman of medium height, now rather overweight, but clearly once beautiful. She takes your goblet aside and fills it from the great bronze mixing-bowl.

If you are in Favour with Dionysus, turn to **286**.
Otherwise, turn to **132**.

562

A silence falls on the company, afraid lest even the slightest sound alert the creature, yet it is no use. It comes, like a dog on the scent of fresh meat after the battle. With one toss of its head it rips off the figurehead of Athena, swallows it whole and turns once again towards the ship. You realize that you have no weapons. Do you go down below to fetch them (**298**), or do you go into battle unarmed (**602**)?

563

If Ares is your patron, go to **329**. Otherwise, go to **445**.

564

The innkeeper, trembling in awe at your brave heart, but relief at mercy clear on his face, shows you to the best room in the inn. Suspicious that he may set about you in the darkness of the night, you sleep lightly and with the door jammed shut with a wedge. In the morning you awake and eat a sumptuous breakfast, served by the innkeeper's daughter. You continue on your journey. Go to **3**.

565

Roll two dice. If this is less than your Might without weapons (but adding 1 for every Honour point you use), then you manage to bring a cow down to the ground, avoiding its man-piercing horns, and one of the oarsmen spears it. It dies, thrashing around in agony, bellowing its defiance to the last (go to **487**). If you fail, take 1 Shame point, and you may either give up the hope of fresh-blooded meat, and return to the ship (go to **323**), try to spear the cow (go to **535**), or try to wrestle another cow (remain at **565**).

566

Swelling up with pride, you boast of your victorious encounter with the traitors. 'Fool,' he says, 'out of your own mouth you convict yourself not only a braggart, but a double murderer. Throw him into the storeroom. Tomorrow we shall deal with him.' Go to **75**.

567

You cannot look for aid here on the far seas in the grip of the deep-running waters of Ocean. Lose 1 Honour point, and return to **547**.

568

You must either sacrifice 6 Honour points to appease Poseidon and go to **424** (if he is your patron he would then aid you), or risk his wrath and go to **257**.

569

Just at the point when grim-faced Despair had almost conquered your spirit, the door opens, and a richly dressed man enters. 'I am Protamios,' he says, 'the steward of King Aegeus. Today is the day of a great feast, and the king himself has ordered that you attend, thinking it disgraceful that a stranger be imprisoned in the palace without a chance to explain himself and share in a meal with the household.'

You must lose 1 Honour point, and go to **350**.

570
The black-clad man does not seem surprised when your broken limbs and bloodied chest mend and are whole. He redoubles his efforts, yet the force behind his assault has weakened, and now he is only Might 7, Protection 12.

If you surrender, go to **121**.
If you retreat, turn to **387**.
If you Seriously Wound your opponent, turn to **519**.

571
You drop your club. Take 1 Shame point, as the combat rules state. Procrustes chains you to the bed, and, try as you may, in your wounded state you cannot escape. You fall into an uneasy sleep. Turn to **500**.

572
As your body's strength fails, and your life is undone, Zeus the life-giver suffuses your limbs with renewed vigour. You may fight on. Return to **124**.

573
You approach the camp. In the distance the campfires glow like huge fireflies. Soon the war will be over. You are cheerful, and there is gladness in your heart. There is some movement in the bushes, but you ignore it.

Another movement stirs the silence of the night, and there before you stands an Amazon in full battle-dress.

Do you try to explain your mission (**563**)?
Do you attack her (**517**)?
Or do you retreat back to the city, and await the battle next morning (**165**)?

574

Legend has it that the oracle at Delphi originated when a goat and goatherd inhaled vapours from a fissure in the hillside, and began to prophesy. Soon a cult of Apollo sprang up there, and the oracle was taken over by the Pythian priestess. The Pythia was originally a young woman, but after one such was ravaged by a client, older women were used as priestesses. The interpretation was carried out by the priests, and the prophecies were generally in hexameter verse, although not of a very high standard.

Have 1 Shame point, and lose 1 Honour point. Return to **554**.

575

You almost shake with joy, as you return to the harbour, that you have recovered the precious letters to Minos. If you had not had them, the wrath of gods and men at your mission's ending would have been as the stormy anger of the Olympians against the earth-built Titans, penned in their fiery tombs as punishment for the destruction wrought upon the fair green world. Go to **475**.

576

Seeing you, the men scatter, like a handful of sand cast into the wind. The sickle-bearer makes a half-hearted attempt to strike at you, but thinks better of it and he too is gone. You turn to pick up the terrified puppy from the altar, but as you do it bites you, and runs off yapping into the fields.

As you start again down the road into the town, the goddess Hecate herself speaks from her altar, 'You have desecrated my altar, Altheus, and the enmity of the goddess is worse than the vengeance of Zeus himself.' With this the voice ceases, and the altar splits from top to bottom. You are now in Disfavour with Hecate. Go to **188**.

577

The sea-serpent is Might 20, Protection 12.

If you attack it, turn to **533**.

If you decide to do nothing, in case the creature has not noticed the ship, turn to **562**.

578

O Cythera, you are fairer by far than the finest flower of Aegeus' garden and the realm of Attica, bedecked in summer's finery; while the breath of the fair goddess soothes all it touches, all is peace.

Yet even in gardens there is a place where a tall cypress casts its shadows, and nothing may grow. You hear shouts and screams. You notice a small boat driven against the life-rending rocks at the beach's edge. A woman shouts out in distress and mortal danger.

Do you jump in, and try to save the woman (**31**)?

Or do you decide not to risk the rocks, and go ashore to meet her (**409**)?

579

The beast, with its little spark of intelligence, thinks you are dead, and leaves you, once more to assault its wooden foe. Splinters fly, and there is screaming. Meanwhile life flows once more in your veins, and you struggle closer to the ship. Go to **381**.

580

Turning to the right, you soon see that a large number of people seem to be making for an open space set like a courtyard between four large buildings. They stand in the colonnade, hushed and seeming to listen to something. When you reach the place, you hear the chanting of a bard, telling the tales of the labours of Herakles.

Do you stand and listen for a while (**434**)?

Or do you carry on walking (**137**)?

581
After your earlier treatment, you are suspicious, and watch Medea as she fills your goblet. You note that she takes some powder from a pocket in her deep-blue robe.

Do you accept the wine and drink (**132**)?
Do you accept the wine, but spill it (**227**)?
Or do you insist the queen drink it herself (**482**)?

582
Your last blow strikes home, and the creature shrieks out in agony, lashes out with its tail, and tries to swim off, its skin of iridescent green now clouded with its dark-red blood. The captain, praising Zeus for deliverance, orders those of the rowers who have survived to get under way. The black-sailed vessel limps onwards to Crete. Have 7 Honour points, and go to **349**.

583

It is now several days since your arrival at Cythera. The ship is as well prepared as the captain can manage with the materials available. Reluctant to risk his vessel, yet spurred on by the responsibility of the task he has undertaken, he decides to set sail once more. The remnants of the sail are hoisted, and they flutter like great black crows in the breeze.

As you get under way the captain entertains you with stories of Talos, the great bronze man of Crete who walks round the island three or four times a day, attacking all those who mean Crete harm. Sometimes it preys on shipping, but no Cretan could kill it, nor would want to.

Crete is not far, and soon you will be at the court of King Minos. Go to **158**.

584

'I will reward you with a service, Altheus. If you ever happen to be dying, I will ensure Zeus hears you.' You may have 2 Honour points, and may call on Zeus to save you one extra time. Go to **146**.

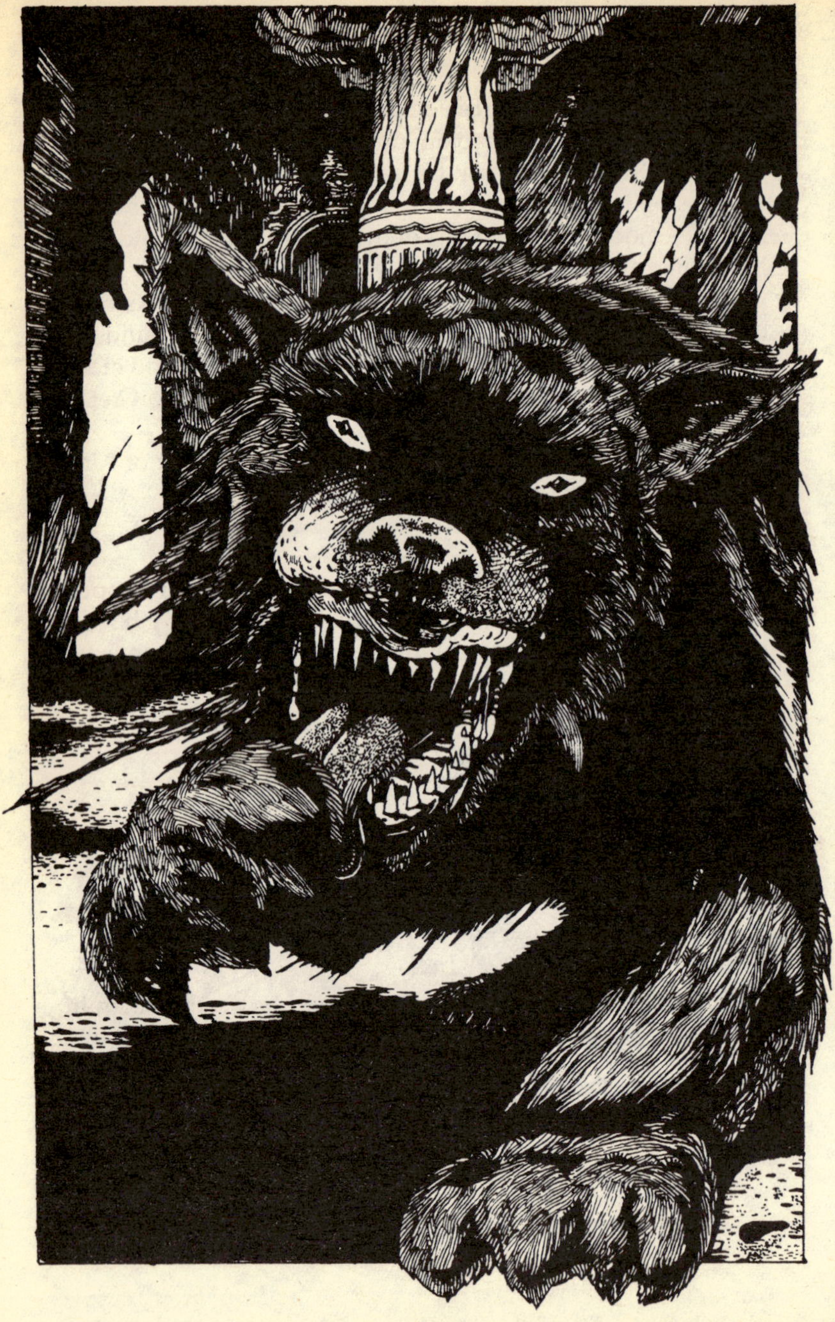

585

You are in a circular chamber from which there appears to be but one exit. In the centre is a circular altar, on the middle of which stands an image of the goddess Hecate, carved in white marble, and triple-formed. Another stands at the entrance, while all is lit with an unearthly glow by three torches set in brackets on the wall. You barely have time to cry out against the injustice of your fate, when there appears, as if from nowhere or from the gates of Hades itself, a huge black puppy, froth-dripping maw filled with needle-sharp teeth, eyes ablaze with a dark fire. It bounds towards you, and attacks. It has Might 8, Protection 17.

If you retreat, go to **147**.
If you are victorious, go to **558**.
If you die, and pray to Zeus, go to **512**.

586

You pick some of the purple grapes and eat them, their juice trickling down your reddened cheeks, and staining your tunic. It is good that Aethra your mother is not here. After a while you feel a cramp in your stomach. Perhaps you ought not to have tasted the vine's refreshing fruit.

You could search for some honey to assuage your hunger further (**276**).

Or you could return to the ship (**595**).

Or you could try to catch one of the cattle, helped by the other sailors (**59**).

587

'You silly boy,' giggles the woman. 'I pity any *real* maiden in distress. You'd better come with me and get out of those wet things.' With this she flicks her wrist, and in a whiff of Tyrian perfume you are transported to the goddess's Cytherean palace. Go to **235**.

588

The swineherd is an athletic youth, and you almost lose him as he rushes off through the tangle of Athens. Quickly you reach a magnificent building with colonnades and arches, and with baskets of flowers adorning the front; this is the palace of your father.

The swineherd does not, however, take you in, but darts away down a side-street. You call out to him, but he does not reply, and you follow him down the alleyway.

He points to a small entrance at the back of the building. From the interior comes a smell of cooking. 'Here it is,' he says, 'the way in.' You begin to feel hungry.

Do you knock (**7**)?

Or do you simply go on in (**270**)?

589

You descend, taking the right-hand path down towards Cenchraea. Only the sound of birdsong disturbs the silence of your journey. Away in the gulf a merchant ship plies its way towards the port, carrying cloths dyed in Tyrian purple to the rich men of the town. As you reach the outermost edge of the town, you see that the merchantman has reached the harbour, and is unloading its goods on the wharf. A crowd of people has gathered close to the ship, eager for passage to the great city of Athens.

Do you join them and try to shorten your journey by taking the sea-route to Athens (go to **68**)?

Or do you choose to take the overland route (go to **455**)?

590

The divine queen hears your prayer, and from the wooded slopes of Cythera she comes, radiant in her beauty. 'Well, Altheus,' she whispers, 'you are a mess. Still I'll see what I can do.' With a flick of her hand your appearance is transformed. No longer do you seem like a bedraggled, travel-worn beggar, but as a true hero, strong and filled with prowess. 'Oh, and by the way,' adds Aphrodite coyly, 'don't drink any wine, it would spoil the effect.' With one last admiring glance at her artistry, the goddess is gone, back to her leafy-gladed home.

When the guards return, they are so astounded at the change in your demeanour that you soon persuade them to escort you to the king's feast, as a guest, not as a prisoner. Go to **350**.

591
Too late. Go to **500**.

592
Bewildered, you step into a side-street, where you slump to the ground in utter despair of finding the palace. Near by you see a tall, grey-eyed, imperious woman. She waits expectantly. When you clamber to your feet she speaks. 'I am Pallas Athena, and this is my city. Go now to the Acwopolis, from where you may see all Athens, and the place you seek.'

If Athena is your patron, go to **91**.

If she is not, then turn to **325**.

593
Whenever you feel that you are able, you may sacrifice 10 Honour points to Zeus. He will then listen to your prayers one extra time. After this the brooch is useless, except as a present, bribe or souvenir. Go to **492**.

594

You soon find somebody willing to part with the small sum you are demanding for the loaf. But you now feel even worse than before, as though branded a criminal. For your heinous acts, take 2 Shame points. You could immediately leave Megara and this shameful incident behind you (go to **86**), or you could go back to the market-place and steal some more, continuing your life of crime (go to **5**).

595

Have 2 Honour points, and go to **323**.

596

Apollo, your patron, stands at the prow of the ship. 'Never mind,' he says. 'Some of us are cowards, but I didn't think you were. Beware women on golden thrones.' Startled by this apparition, you look up to the heavens, but when you turn your gaze back, he is gone. Perhaps you have offended him. Turn to **492**.

597

Boldly you traverse the battlefield, seeking opponents, whose life-blood might be spilt against the keen edge of your sword. Yet there are none, only the dead and dying; all those Amazons who were able to have fled back to their ships and their far-off land at the edge of Ocean's great river. Yet many young Athenians have died this day, and it is with sorrow in your heart and regret that, though a hero, you have fought but little, that you return to Aegeus' palace. Go to **283**.

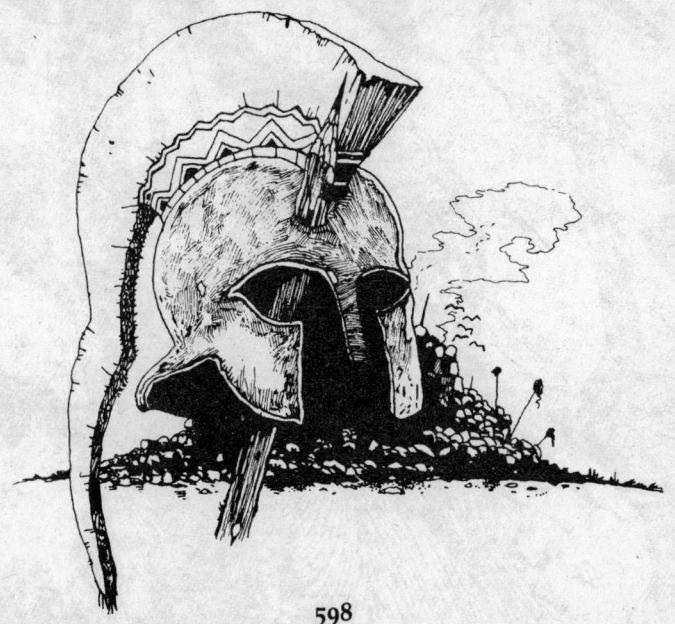

598

In your frenzied hurry you nearly dived in with all your armour. Stripping down to your loincloth, you plunge in. As you are not a strong swimmer, you take ten minutes to cover the hundred yards or so to the boat. You take hold of it, and almost by a miracle it seems immensely light, as the feathers of the birds which fly high above the care-worn earth. The woman smiles sweetly. 'My hero! You have rescued me.'

If Aphrodite is your patron, turn to **557**.

Otherwise, turn to **141**.

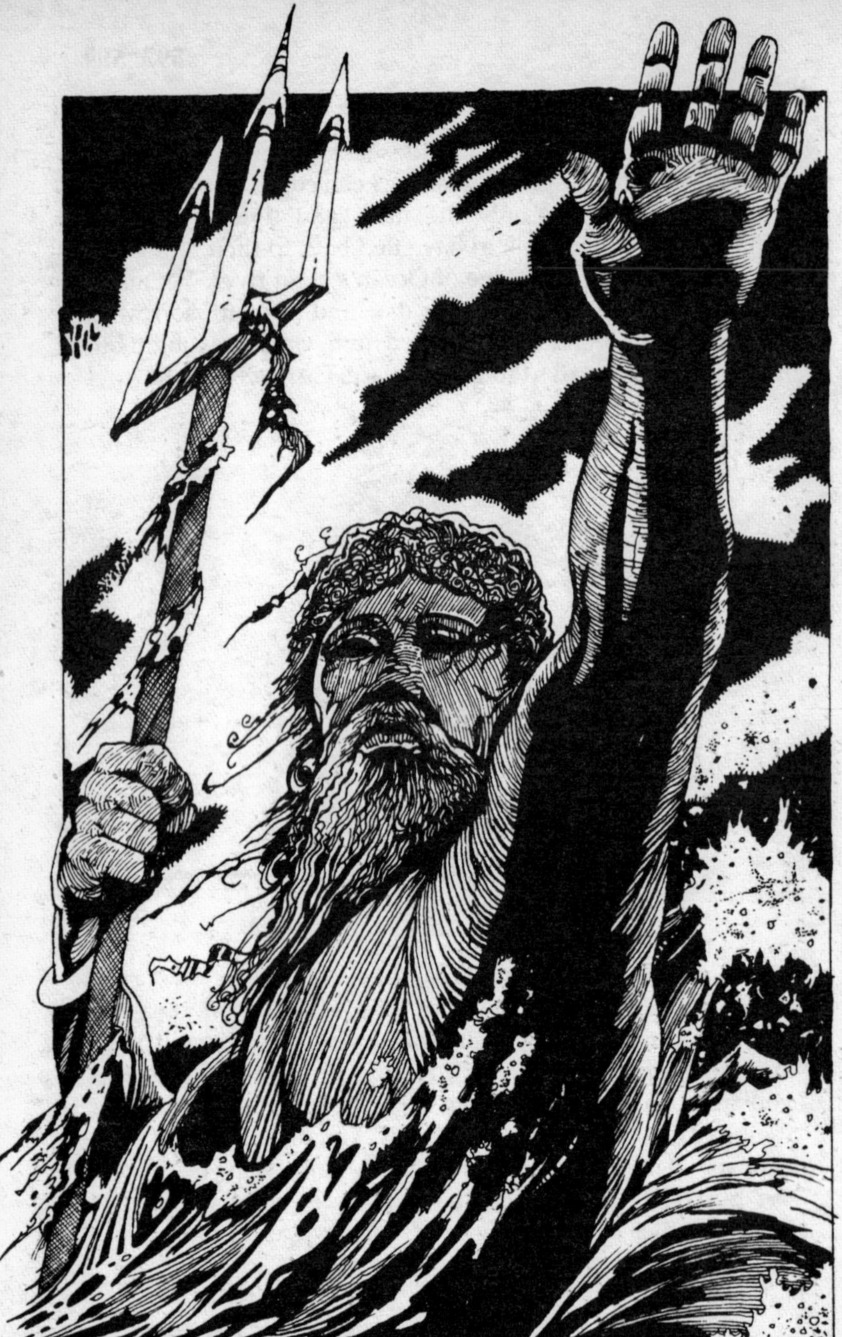

599

Poseidon, lord of the oceans, arises from his depths, trident in hand, glory radiating from the very waters that fall from his back. He raises a conch shell to his lips and blows. At the sound of its master the beast whines, coils its tail around its neck, submerges and is gone.

'Altheus,' booms Poseidon, 'afraid of my little pet? Still, you always did scare more easily than Theseus. Watch you don't disturb anything later on, but then I suppose they might not eat heroes.'

With a last sarcastic glance, Poseidon is gone, back to the feast with the daughters of Ocean from which you disturbed him. The crew, captain and Athenians are amazed at your summoning of the god. Hopes raised, the oarsmen go back to their benches, glad that they have a true hero aboard, but perplexed at the words of the god. Go to **349**.

600

'We will never surrender,' says the leader, and as he does, they impale themselves on their knives. You may have 5 Honour points, and you carry on towards the temple, wondering at the ways of men. Go to **216**.

601

You set about the man, but it is soon clear that the greybeard will not defend himself, and will not even try to flee. Perhaps he has some hidden weapon or poisoned ring.

Do you leave him, with a threat to kill him if he follows (**430**)?

Or do you kill him before he can do you harm, steal the ship's food or surprise you at night (**530**)?

602

While you hesitated, one of the crew members has thrown a harpoon at the beast, but it missed. You snatch up a sharp knife (Might 1, Protection 0) from the deck and prepare to face the creature.

Do you dive into the water to attack (**361**)?

Or do you consider that the ship is a safer point from which to strike at the serpent (**484**)?

603

The throne of Knossos is gypsum, and has a griffin carved on either side. Have 1 Shame point and go to **158**.

604

'Pyraphas,' she mumbles, as if trying to remember something. Then she seems to remember. 'Ah! You must be here to help at the feast,' she booms. 'Well, you don't look much help. Go over there and clean those mixing-bowls – haven't been used since Aegeus married Medea.' With this, you are dispatched into a corner, and set to work. Such labour is demeaning, but you see that this feast must be a lavish one indeed, for all day meat, bread and wine are brought in by servants from the pastures and fields around the palace. Go to **234**.

605

You pray to your patron god, craving succour from the wrath of Hecate. To be saved from the infernal creature you must sacrifice 2 Honour points to your patron, and 3 to Hecate.

If you cannot, or are unwilling to make the sacrifice, go to **585**.

If you do sacrifice the Honour points, go to **458**.

606
You lose your strike, and it is now the Amazon's turn to attack; her ears are clearly closed by the mad fury that comes from Ares. Return to **517**, and continue the combat.

607
Full of confidence, you grasp the urn firmly, lift it to your lips and drink deeply. Lowering the urn you are horrified to see that, instead of giving you the rapturous reception you expected, the crowd are booing and jeering. Go to **120**.

608
Wondering at the will of the gods, you wander along the sands of Cythera, looking for a spot to rest while the ship is repaired. You will need to build a shelter from the plentiful branches and remains of earlier wrecks. The crew is busy with the ship, and the young men and maidens, avoiding both you and the captain, have gone in the opposite direction. You are alone, therefore, when you see a man dressed in oil-stained rags, his hair white, eyes wild and beard unkempt. He too catches sight of you, and runs along the strand towards you. Too stunned to react, you do not move, and the old man, perhaps a native of these parts, perhaps a survivor of some wreck, begins to rant incoherently.

Do you attack him in case he becomes violent (**601**)?

Or do you stay and try to understand what he is saying (**418**)?

609
No hero should be afraid of crowds. Does the very sight of the sea make you sicken? Take 1 Shame point, and return to **589**.

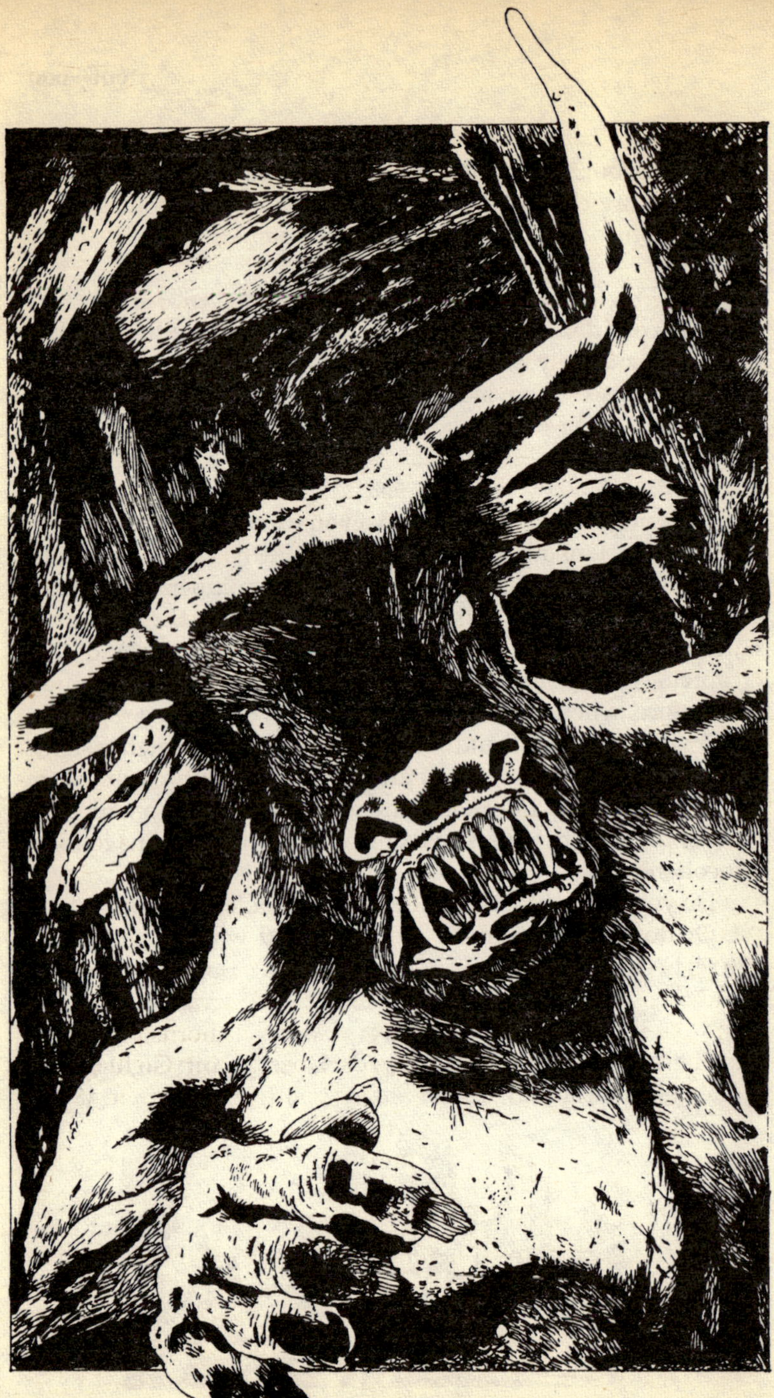

610
The man looks at your brooch with disdain, and says, 'Your bet's on blue, it's the only one left.' Go to **391**.

611
You sit content, watching as another great-prowed vessel comes into the harbour, offloading its goods for the Cythneans. There is a storm in the distance, perhaps near cursed Ceos, and the wind increases to roaring thunder, while the lightning blazes in defiance against the waters. Wood is brought to repair the ship, but soon you sleep, exhausted by your trials. On awakening, you find that the captain and crew have gathered, while the Athenian youths and maidens, solemn-faced in their garlands and flowers, have returned from the place where they have spent the day, perhaps one of their last, if amicable Altheus cannot fulfil his task. Go to **475**.

612
You seem to be in a dark corridor. A torch in the bracket on one wall casts a baleful light, but only reveals the passage stretching endlessly onwards, punctuated by openings to the left and right. Further and further you wander, frantically seeking to escape from whatever place the forces of darkness have cast you into. From time to time you hear a sound like footsteps, and hurry faster, as the man who thinks his enemies follow but can never turn round lest he confront them.

Something shiny glints in a corner. You stoop to pick it up, and hear a great roaring from behind. You scramble around and see there a great bull-headed creature, its horns poised to tear out your throat and your great hearted spirit. Go to **337**.

613
You are ready for battle, but the Amazons are not prepared to risk any of their number. As you leave the tent, you are seized by some eight of them, whom your erstwhile opponent has taken the opportunity of summoning. All your weapons are taken from you, but you are allowed to return to Athens unhindered. Lose 1 Honour point, and go to **320**.

614

You wish that you could light the lamp, but this would surely bring the innkeeper to investigate. What little you can make out is as the islands in the vast wine-dark realms of Ocean.

'. . . Storm-tossed Ceos . . .'

'. . . who died from eating of Poseidon's Melian herd . . .'

'. . . Never aid a lame man . . .'

There is a clash, as of a massive shield in the bitter battle. Someone is coming. You must leave for the ship. Have 1 Shame point for your action and go to **575**.

615

You may have 6 Honour points for defeating the sow, and, in addition, one of the grateful citizens of Crommyon gives you a spear for delivering them. It is Might 3, Protection 1. Go to **378**.

616

Leaving the sounds of the revel far behind, you press on into the forest. The undergrowth is dense here, and the moon is now hidden behind a blanket of clouds. An owl hoots in the distance. Suddenly you are knocked sprawling by a blow from in front. At first you think you must have walked into an overhanging branch, but soon you realize that you face a live adversary, a bear. You have no choice but to defend yourself. The bear is Might 6, Protection 13.

If you are victorious, turn to **526**.

If you retreat, go to **210** (remembering to lose 1 Honour point even if you fail in the attempt).

If you die and are saved by Zeus turn to **362**.

617

With one last blow you topple the metal Titan. His bronze body creaks and groans, sways forward towards the ship, and falls, screaming hellishly, to the shallows of the sea. Yet from his mouth there still exudes his fiery breath. Perhaps only the Olympian gods can destroy him. In any case, have 8 Honour points and go to **384**.

618

You are stunned at the scenes of chaos, as the dazed and confused charioteers are led from their vehicles. Several of the horses are dead; one of the charioteers is screaming horribly. Only the yellow driver is unscathed. You go over to the wounded red driver, but he refuses to return your bet, as no one has won. Scowling, you spit on the ground, and call on Zeus to witness this deed. You would have shown the man the rewards of crossing amicable Altheus, but it is shameful to strike a wounded man. Inwardly you regret that you ever gave such a valuable gift. You return to your inn, as the rest of the races are cancelled, sleep the night there, and go on to Athens next morning (**474**).

619

Storm-battered and sea-stained, bruised by the relentless swell, you lose hold of your possessions. You lose one piece of armour (of your choice), one weapon and one other item from your Chronicle Sheet, which must not be armour or weapons. You may not lose the documents for Minos, or anything of Antiope's. Note that if you possess only one item in any of these categories, you need not lose it. For example, if you have only one piece of armour, you may keep it. Go to **363**.

620

Kindly wonder at the ways of men in private, and don't bother the gods. Their death is enough. Have 1 Shame point and go to **216**.

in preparation:

Cretan Chronicles 2:
AT THE COURT OF KING MINOS (late 1985)

Cretan Chronicles 3:
RETURN OF THE WANDERER (spring 1986)

The Fighting Fantasy Gamebooks in Puffin:

1. THE WARLOCK OF FIRETOP MOUNTAIN
2. THE CITADEL OF CHAOS
3. THE FOREST OF DOOM
4. STARSHIP TRAVELLER
5. CITY OF THIEVES
6. DEATHTRAP DUNGEON
7. ISLAND OF THE LIZARD KING
8. SCORPION SWAMP
9. CAVERNS OF THE SNOW WITCH
10. HOUSE OF HELL
11. TALISMAN OF DEATH
12. SPACE ASSASSIN
13. FREEWAY FIGHTER
14. TEMPLE OF TERROR
15. THE RINGS OF KETHER
16. SEAS OF BLOOD

MAELSTROM
Alexander Scott

Imagine a band of travellers on the long road from St Albans to London – a dangerous journey in troubled times. YOU choose the characters you play, YOU decide the missions and YOU have the adventures in the turbulent world of Europe in the sixteenth century – either as a player or as the referee.

Complete with Beginners' and Advanced Rules, Referee's Notes, maps, charts and a solo adventure to get you started, *Maelstrom* is a great game for three or more players.

FIGHTING FANTASY
The introductory Role-playing game
Steve Jackson

The world of fighting Fantasy, people by Orcs, dragons, zombies and vampires, has captured the imagination of millions of readers world-wide. Thrilling adventures of sword and sorcery come to life in the Fighting Fantasy Gamebooks, where the reader is the hero, dicing with death and demons in search of villains, treasure or freedom.

Now YOU can create your own Fighting Fantasy adventures and send your friends off on dangerous missions! In this clearly written handbook, there are hints on devising combats, monsters to use, tricks and tactics, as well as two mini-adventures complete with Games-Master's notes for you to start with. Literally countless adventures await you!

WHAT IS DUNGEONS AND DRAGONS?
John Butterfield, Philip Parker, David Honigmann

A fascinating guide to the greatest of all role-playing games: it includes detailed background notes, hints on play and dungeon design, strategy and tactics, and will prove invaluable for players and beginners alike.

Steve Jackson's

SORCERY!

1. THE SHAMUTANTI HILLS

Your search for the legendary Crown of Kings takes you to the Shamutanti Hills. Alive with evil creatures, lawless wanderers and bloodthirsty monsters, the land is riddled with tricks and traps waiting for the unwary traveller. Will you be able to cross the hills safely and proceed to the second part of the adventure – or will you perish in the attempt?

2. KHARÉ – CITYPORT OF TRAPS

As a warrior relying on force of arms, or a wizard trained in magic, you must brave the terror of a city built to trap the unwary. You will need all your wits about you to survive the unimaginable horrors ahead and to make sense of the clues which may lead to your success – or to your doom!

3. THE SEVEN SERPENTS

Seven deadly and magical serpents speed ahead of you to warn the evil Archmage of your coming. Will you be able to catch them before they get there?

4. THE CROWN OF KINGS

At the end of your long trek, you face the unknown terrors of the Mampang Fortress. Hidden inside the keep is the Crown of Kings – the ultimate goal of the *Sorcery!* epic. But beware! For if you have not defeated the Seven Serpents, your arrival has been anticipated . . .

Complete with all the magical spells you will need, each book can be played either on its own, or as part of the whole epic.